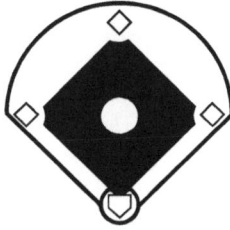

PLAYED

By Juan I. Catalan

PLAYED

Juan I. Catalan

ISBN 978-1-968149-00-0

Joint Venture Publishing

The Millionaire Mentor, Inc.

JMP

JOINT VENTURE

PUBLISHING

Written transcript of the broadcast of the May 12, 2003, game at Dodger Stadium is reprinted with permission from the Los Angeles Dodgers.

Printed in the United States of America

Imagery by Oscar

JUAN CATALAN

DEDICATION

To all the Longshots who never gave up.

For every kid who thought they couldn't amount to anything.

For every person who was dismissed, written off, or falsely accused.

This book is for you: You can live through the worst of the worst...
and still rise.

JUAN CATALAN

CONTENTS

JUAN CATALAN

INTRODUCTION
By Todd Melnik

Just take a moment to think about the nightmare scenario you are about to read—because it could happen to you.

Imagine yourself being arrested by a SWAT team at gunpoint in front of your young children. Then you aren't told what you were arrested for by anyone for over 6 hours. Then you learn you are facing the death penalty for an assassination you did not commit, only to get to court and learn you are being prosecuted by a government lawyer who never lost a murder case and was given the nickname Sniper for picking off people "legally" with the death penalty.

This is the true-life story of Juan Catalan, expanding well beyond the critically-acclaimed and Emmy-nominated Netflix documentary, Long Shot. It's a story of faith, purpose, perseverance, struggle, and ultimately the validation of a life previously unknown.

Without his faith and quite literally multiple miracles that came together to exonerate Juan, all of which are now the basis for his captivating motivational speaking engagements today, he would be sitting on Death Row, caged like an animal and unable to share this story.

Enjoy this story of my good friend, Juan Catalan.

Todd L. Melnik
Law Offices of Todd L. Melnik
Woodland Hills, CA

CHAPTER ONE

THE GRAPE

*H*i, everybody, and a very pleasant good evening to you, wherever you may be. We are at Dodger Stadium, where it is a beautiful evening as we await the start of the first meeting of the year between the Atlanta Braves and the Dodgers. The Dodger's players are running out to their position accompanied by youngsters. Autographs will be given, and then it'll be time to go to work for Hideo Nomo and the home team ball club. The Dodgers are two games above .500 at home, they're break even on the road, and they come home two games above and six games behind the Giants. The Dodgers will be looking north at PNC Park to see what goes on at Pacific Bell, and up there the Giants are the National League's best team in the first game of a series. They have won nine and lost three, so we'll be watching what they do with the Expos because San Francisco has won twelve of the last eighteen meetings against Montreal.

Vin Scully, Dodger's Stadium, May 12, 2003

Have you ever been accused of something you didn't do—what was it?

Maybe your family thought you were the one who ate the last tamale that was supposed to be for your abuelita? Or possibly your coworkers believed that you were the one who spread the lie that got Luis fired?

If you were innocent, you would want to tell anyone who'd listen...

But, more important, you would want to yell out, I didn't do that! Believe me, I didn't do that.

Now, take this same scenario but take it up a notch. You are now being accused of MURDER. To make things worse, capital murder that carries a death penalty sentence. Now picture yourself screaming, I did not do this! Please believe me, I did not do this.

That's what happened to me.

If you've seen the Netflix documentary, LONG SHOT, you know a little about my case.

> Long Shot is a 2017 short documentary film about how Juan Catalan was arrested for a murder he did not commit. A TV show, Curb Your Enthusiasm, contains raw footage that was instrumental in proving his innocence.

But you know very little about me. So that's what this book is for.

My name is Juan Ignacio Catalan. The story I'm going to tell you centers around one specific baseball game—a game I was never even supposed to be at—the Dodgers game that changed and saved my life and cleared my name of murder. It was the love of a game that became a miracle—but not the only miracle—the lucky break. But for all the reasons that led up to it, I was there.

And sometimes in life, just being there is enough. Sometimes being there is all you need. And on that specific day, being in the stands, sitting next to my daughter, buying her cotton candy and popcorn, and buying myself a Dodgers' hat was enough to get me out of jail, to have my name cleared, to allow me to see my family again, and to begin building the amazing life I now get to tell you about.

And all I had to do that day was just show up to that game. Just be there. Watching the Dodgers, enjoying the day with my family and friends, just doing that—would be enough.

I have a lot to tell you. All of it good. All of it true, And all of it enough.

There are many stories of enough in my life, so let's start with one of those.

My mother tells of such a story that happened when I was three years old and my father brought home a bag of green grapes. She gave me a few and then walked into the kitchen. When she got there, she felt an intuition that made her turn around—she said she felt as if something told her to check on me, so she stopped what she was doing and walked back into the living room. When she did, she saw me on the floor turning blue, silently choking from the grape that was stuck in my throat.

My mother ran over and stuck her middle finger down my throat, just enough to push this grape through. She said I instantly started breathing again. The incredible part of this story is that my mom is probably the worst person in an emergency. She panics and starts yelling hysterically. But on that day, my mom did just enough to save my life.

My mother, Magdalena Ortega, was born in Uruapan, Mexico. Having only reached the second grade, I don't know if her parents thought that was enough education for her, or they thought it was not important enough, so they just stopped sending her to school. That was a different type of enough. I know there was other additional childhood trauma back in Mexico—my mother never talked about it, but I know it was there—and whatever it was, it scarred her for life. We saw it in many ways, but the biggest form was the crippling anxiety and fear that she carried.

When I was growing up, my mother would have dizzy and fainting spells, and there was even a two-year period when she absolutely believed she was paralyzed, even though every medical test, every scan, every exam she went through came back negative. You're fine, Magdelena, You're fine. But that didn't matter. My mother believed she had become physically paralyzed—so she was paralyzed. The power of the mind.

My father was not exactly supportive of my mother during this time. My brother and I would watch him scream at her in frustration, wanting her, ordering her, to stop and get up and move and work— mostly work, because that is how my father judged everything. To him, how much work a person did determined their value.

I was angry at my father because he could get enraged, he was mostly impatient, and because he did not know or care what she was going through. Well, I mean, none of us did, I guess, but we still loved her.

Now what's funny is, as I write this, I see the irony in that statement about my dad. Because I judged my father then without knowing any of what he had gone through. So, I was guilty of exactly what I was accusing him of doing.

I knew only the basics of my dad's childhood. That he was born in Guerrero, Mexico in 1946, that's pretty much it. But I did not know that he was forced to go to work at the age of seven. I did not know that his father, my grandfather, would drink often and ignore his family duties, so my father, still a child, had to work hard to bring in enough money to help feed his mother and younger brothers and sisters. My father never told us this, possibly because of shame, I'm not sure, but that is what he did. And when my father brought that little money in each week, my grandfather probably didn't even realize it. It makes me think about what abuse a seven-year-old child had to endure—a kid who was forced to be a man, the child trying to fill the void of his own father.

Like I said, I didn't know any of this at the time because my father never told us. I guess that telling stories like that—and like the one I'm telling you now—would have shown weakness, and Mario Catalan was not a weak man. And he didn't want his sons to be weak, either. I do know that my parents met in Uruapan, Mexico, where my mom is from. They dated—I'm not really sure what that consisted of in 1977 in Mexico—and then my father brought my mother to the US. For my mom, the fact that she was now in an unknown part of the world had to be a culture shock compared to where she had lived. One day, she was on this tiny Mexican farm in the middle of nowhere, and the next, she was in one of the most densely populated areas of the US, just outside of Los Angeles.

My mom, insecure with her second-grade education and small grasp of the world, did the best she could to adapt. She became a mom at the age of 21 with the birth of my brother, and then a year later, she became a mom again with me. It would take my parents another ten years later to officially become husband and wife.

My life began in California. I was born in Los Angeles, but grew up in Sun Valley, which is where my brother and I began school, while my mother was becoming more anxious and my father more upset with her for it.

Life went on, I was about to start kindergarten, but my parents missed the registration cutoff date at my local school, so I had to live with my godparents, who were also my aunt and uncle, for about a year, because the school was down the street from their house and I could get in. My godparents were great. My aunt was like a second mother, and I learned a lot during the time I lived with them. But I did miss my family.

Looking back and being a father now, I cannot understand how my parents could be okay with me living away from them. I mean, I was loved and taken care of by my godparents, but at five years old, that feeling of abandonment still creeps in. And they did not do this with my brother, so I felt that maybe they loved him more.

School was okay. There, I was introduced to bullies. I rarely got a haircut, and I mixed up the few clothes I had to spread what I had out. But the one thing I couldn't do was hide my lisp. That lisp alone was just enough to draw negative attention, even if the clothes and hair didn't do the job. But my teachers were nice.

I transferred from that school to another, and then another. In fact, I attended four different schools in a seven-year span. I went to Pre-K in Tujunga, then kindergarten in Lake View Terrace, first and second grade at Arminta Elementary in Sun Valley, and then I went to Blythe Elementary in Reseda for third and fourth grade. And in the fourth grade, I won a class project, and the prize was a Happy Meal for lunch.

I couldn't believe it! I was so excited. My teacher, Mrs. Gold, brought me my Happy Meal in front of the whole school, and although I felt proud, I hated all the attention that came with it. Having lived a rough childhood, it was times like this that reminded me of God's goodness in my life. I felt special but was not sure how to handle it. I tried to ignore it but could not and ended up giving everything in the Happy Meal away, except the fries.

Mr. Wilby from Arminta Elementary was the first teacher to compliment my writing skills. We had an essay contest in fifth grade, and when I won it, Mr. Wilby read my essay out loud to the class. Again, I was honored to have been chosen but absolutely hated the attention it brought. But this was also around the time that I began to become interested in organized sports.

I am going to talk a lot about sports in this book, because it is a big part of me and my story. Sports became everything to me. Everything good in the world revolved around sports.

I played two seasons of tee-ball when I was a kid, then moved up to two seasons of Little League baseball. I was an All-Star in tee-ball, and I almost made the All-Star team in Little League, but my friend, Miguel, beat me out for the slot.

I have great memories of baseball, except for two things. My coach had his son on the team, who was my friend, and an older son was helping to coach us. He was a good kid who died in an accident involving a firearm. I remember feeling so sad for my friend, my coach, and the entire family. And only weeks later, one of our other teammates was killed in an accident involving a water heater explosion. The realization of death is numbing. And I guess it implanted in me the idea that everything I have all around me can be taken away quickly.

For a long time, baseball was the biggest part of my sports life—until I discovered basketball. Man, I loved playing basketball, at school, at home, at my cousins' house, ALL the time.

This was when I learned about Magic Johnson and the Los Angeles Lakers. And the Lakers became, well, everything to me. When the playoffs occurred, I would lock myself in the room and pray to God that the Lakers would win. I'd speak words of encouragement to the Magic Johnson poster on my wall. For the first time in my life, I had a dream: to play for the Los Angeles Lakers! I could not get enough of the game. I played day and night and dreamed and followed and talked about the Los Angeles Lakers. I was obsessed.

Magic Johnson is one of the greatest basketball players to ever play the game, and his nickname, "Magic," was exactly what you saw when he was on the court. I remember the day our P.E. teacher, Mr. Shine, holding back tears, told us that Magic had tested positive for HIV. I didn't really know what HIV meant, and some of the bigger kids were saying mean things about it, but I didn't care. I loved Magic, and I bought a replica jersey and wore it proudly because Magic belonged to all of us in Los Angeles. He was one of us. He was ours.

As a kid, idolizing Magic was one thing, but I never thought I would actually get to meet arguably the greatest point guard to ever play in the NBA. That day was July 31, 2013, and my cousin, Jimmy, came to visit us from Atlanta. The Yankees were in town, so a bunch of us cousins took him to the game. It was a pitchers' duel with Hiroki Kuroda pitching for the Yankees and Clayton Kershaw on the mound for the Dodgers. The Yankees scored 3 in the 9th inning and won the game 3-0. The next morning, Jimmy had a flight to catch right before noon, so I picked him up and took him to Roscoe's Chicken & Waffles in Hollywood for breakfast. As we ate, we kept talking about the Dodgers game from the day before.

Jimmy is just as big as a baseball fan as me, so we could talk about it for hours. After I paid the check, we walked outside and kept talking. Right about that time, the restaurant manager came outside and asked how our meal was. I told him that Roscoe's was one of my favorite places and that I brought my cousin, who was visiting from Atlanta, to try it. He must've appreciated my response because he was excited to tell us that Magic Johnson was inside eating at the restaurant. "MAGIC JOHNSON IS INSIDE?" I literally yelled. "SSSSHHHHHH! Keep it down," he said in a panic. But he continued, softly to avoid attracting attention, "You didn't hear it from me, but he's inside eating."

Oh, boy, I was beyond excited! I told Jimmy that we had to go back in. "Follow me," I told him as I took the lead. Now, at this particular Roscoe's, they had added a new dining area to the original dining area, which was actually very small. Before they added the new area, there was sometimes an hour's wait for a table. It was crowded when we walked in, and as I scanned the area, I didn't see Magic anywhere. Disappointed, it even occurred to me that the manager had been messing with us. Then, as I was walking toward the bathroom, I looked to my left and there was Magic, sitting in an inside corner! I was so nervous I didn't know what to do, so I continued to walk into the bathroom with Jimmy on my heels. Like a little kid, I was game planning as we walked, telling Jimmy that Magic was right there and that we had to go up to him. "I'm not going up to him, man!" Jimmy said nervously. I replied, "Don't worry, Jimmy, I will. Just follow me." Now, mind you, Magic had become a part owner of the Dodgers just a year earlier in 2012, and Jimmy and I still had our Dodgers gear on from the night before. When we walked out, I looked at Magic, who was staring right at me. I couldn't believe it! What came next was even crazier. Magic Johnson looked at me, pointed his finger, at me and nodded his head! I froze on the spot. Before I could stumble toward him or say a word, he stood up and said, "You guys got on the right gear. Come on, let's take a picture. Larry (someone he was with) come on, get up and take our picture." I nearly passed out. We took the picture, and he thanked us for being fans and shook our hands. I was so nervous that I forgot to tell him about my poster of him in my room and that he was the MAIN reason I fell in love with basketball. As we walked out of there, it was like, "Did that really just happen?" Jimmy's face in the picture says it all, haha.

My brother and I made a homemade backboard in our parents' house, and we played basketball all the time. I remember buying videos and shoes that supposedly helped you to jump higher, basically anything that would make me play better. Slowly, my game improved, and I even ended up joining a park recreation league with my cousin when I was around 15 years of age. My eventual coach told me after a scrimmage tryout game that I had good skills and a good game, but when it came time for the actual game, I stepped back. I was not confident playing in front of people, and my game showed it. I was basically just a body out there, running back and forth without really making a positive contribution to my team. Total lack of confidence, for sure.

After I graduated from sixth grade, I attended Sun Valley Jr. High. I was a good student and tried my best to be outgoing, but it was hard. Since I lacked confidence and self-esteem, I was always hard on myself for making mistakes, and I had a tendency to overanalyze and replay mistakes over and over in my head.

Junior high was my introduction to gangs. I always wondered what made those kids act this way. They seemed like they were not worried or didn't give a shit about anything. I often tried to make sense of it, but I couldn't.

Insofar as family, I became close to my cousin, Miguel. His dad, my

Tio Tomas, was my favorite uncle. When the world made me feel like an outsider, my Tio made me feel like I belonged. Instantly. He always wanted to do big family gatherings and include everyone, and I was just drawn into his personality, or vibe as it's known today. Tio Tomas was also a huge sports fan, and if that was not the source of where my love of sports came from, it sure fueled it. My Tio always wanted his two sons in sports, and he probably talked my dad into also signing me and my brother up. I don't really remember my dad cheering us on, but I do remember my uncle leading the cheers. My Tio was a constant at my cousins' games, and when he could, he would watch my games and my brother's games. He took us kids to our first soccer game and our first Dodgers game, where we sat in the Top Deck, sharing his binoculars one by one to watch Fernando "El Toro" Valenzuela pitch. That rubbed off on me, as well, as I am always trying to put together sporting events or trips with my friends and family. My Tio had a huge heart, as well. One year, when my dad went to Mexico, my mom and us kids were left at home, and because my mom never learned to drive, we were without a car. It was a Friday afternoon, and I was lying on the couch and heard a horn honk. At first, I didn't pay attention, but the honking did not stop, so I got up and looked out the door. It was my uncle, and he waved for me to come to the car. When I walked up to his door, he handed me a bag with a bucket of ice cream. I was speechless.

It was just a small thing but one that I never forgot. That was my Tio Tomas.

My Tio was the best. My dad and uncle worked together here in the U.S for more than ten years. And in the beginning of 1990, they decided to go into business for themselves. The family machine shop was born, and they could not have been happier. The shop ran great with both of them, but only for a few months. That's when my uncle was diagnosed with cancer. A few months after that, at the age of 44, my dad lost his closest brother and was left with a brand-new business, not knowing if it would survive.

My aunt and cousins were devastated with his passing, as we all were. That was my first time losing someone so close to me, and it affected me very much. I think this is when my anxiety kicked in.

Not having an idea of what anxiety was, I thought something was seriously wrong with me. I didn't have anyone to talk to. I was trapped with these negative feelings with no escape. It wasn't until I met

Alma that I temporarily forgot all about the anxiety. Alma was in my biology class in high school in the tenth grade. I thought she was so pretty, but for a long time I thought this from afar. Very afar. Again, because of my lack of confidence or self-esteem, I would have never approached her. Then one day, I sort of did. And from then on, Alma and I talked all the time at school and then after on the phone. For the first time in my life, I fell in love. I only wanted to be with her, and we were seldom apart.

Alma loved Tweety birds, so any spare money I had went to purchasing anything with a Tweety bird on it.

When my dad bought a new truck, I would wait for him to go to sleep and take his keys. I would drive to Alma's house and take her out, quietly slipping back into our house later. And when Alma and I were eighteen, we had our names tattooed on each other.

Growing up Mexican in Los Angeles is different than it is in most other places. We lived in Sun Valley, which is mostly made up of Hispanics, with some white and Asian families sprinkled in. My godparents, who I stayed with for a year when I was a kid, lived in a predominantly black neighborhood. My cousins had almost all black friends, and we got to know them, as well.

One time, my entire family and I were leaving my godparents' house. We turned the corner, and there was a large group of black teenage kids in the middle of the street. When my dad patiently waited for them to move and they did not, he honked the horn. As the crowd started to separate enough for us to drive through, one of the kids kicked in one of the doors on my dad's station wagon. Being just 7 or 8 years old, that scared me. I believe a lot of what one thinks of another race has a lot to do with your specific experiences with that race. This was a negative one, but later in my life, it would be a black deputy sheriff who possibly saved my life.

Life went on, and so did school. And at the beginning of each school year, the teacher would ask what I did over the summer. I would lie, or at least twist the truth a bit. The lie went something like this...

"We go to Mexico," I'd answer, and then I'd tell stories of visiting beautiful towns and the beaches we explored. That was my answer. And it was a lie. Telling the truth—that we did not do much or that we actually went to Mexico to work on my grandfather's farm—doesn't sound as fun. Because it was not.

Sheffield threw on the fly right by the box seats 330 feet away, going out to get it was Javy Lopez. And so Green came in behind him. So McGriff a line drive double to right with Green able to hustle in with two down and score, and boy did Sheffield really let that thing fly. But not in time; it got by Lopez briefly. However, McGriff was into second standing, and we have a 1-1 tie and the batter now is Brian Jordan. So Reynolds was fortunate that Sheffield caught the ball hit by LoDuca, and the fastball is off the plate and the count one ball and no strikes. So Nomo is even, 1-1 here in the first inning. Brian Jordan with that bruised hand, hitting .299, three homeruns, seventeen runs batted in. He has two home runs in the past against Reynolds, this time a groundball to short, Furcal is up with it throws him out and that's that. But the Dodgers bounce right back. A walk to Green and a double for McGriff and at the end of an inning a 1-1 tie.

Vin Scully, Dodger's Stadium, May 12, 2003

CHAPTER TWO

HORSING AROUND

S econd inning in a 1-1 tie and Robert Fick will start it off. A local boy who lives in Manhattan Beach and went to Cal State Northridge. Big left-hand batter 6' 1" 195. Nomo twists and turns over the top fastball strike, and the count 0 and 1. Robert originally a number five pick by the Tigers back in 1996. He's the youngest in a family of eight children: six boys, two girls, and they all played sports. Here's the strike one pitch on the way to Robert, and he takes high one and one. His brother, Chuck, is a cross checker, a scout in other words, for the Saint Louis Cardinals. And two of Rob's brothers played minor league baseball. Even at the age of fourteen, he was involved with a bat doing an ad for Gatorade. The one-one pitch and Fick takes high ball two, two and one. A very persistent fella and when people asked about his persistence, he put it this way, he took his wife, Jennifer, to the senior prom and then became engaged after going together for ten years. Here's the two-one pitch and Robert check swings slow roller going to be a tough play for somebody it's Beltre who throws it away!

Vin Scully, Dodger's Stadium, May 12, 2003

My grandfather's farm was in Guerrero, Mexico. It was as rural as rural can be, even the neighboring villages were just a collection of houses surrounded by the mountains. It was nature at its finest. It was organic 20 years before I knew what organic meant. My grandfather's farm was run down, but it was still one of the nicest places in that area and the village beyond. It also contained more livestock than several of the nearby farms combined, so in that part of the world, my grandfather was a pretty big deal. My Tio Ignacio (Nacho) and my Tia Maria also lived in the village. Tio Nacho was the oldest of the males and was in charge of the farm as my grandfather was getting older. My Tia Maria looked after my grandmother well into their late life and did the cooking and cleaning for them.

Now, my brother, Mario, and my cousins, Luis, and Robert, loved going to my grandfather's place each year and would get excited weeks before—maybe because they were a little older so they had lots of friends and traveled around the surrounding villages to go to most festivals and dances. I'm not sure. But I knew that I hated it. As soon as we got there, I would begin to count the days until we could go back home.

People always ask about the food when I tell this part of the story, but I have to admit that I did not like it. I mean, it was all fresh, grass-fed meat with freshly made milk and cheese. We ate chicken soup, carnitas, fresh beef, fresh eggs, venison, and iguana. Besides the iguana, those foods are delicacies here in the US. But I would have traded it all for a hamburger or a slice of pizza.

The food was a small part of our time there; the majority of it seemed to be work. Even as little kids, the days were pretty much the same. We were in the fields picking corn, peanuts, and a plant called zorgo that was fed to the animals. After that, we would help tend to the animals, and there were many of them. There were cows, bulls, horses, mules, donkeys, pigs, turkeys, chickens, and goats. We helped feed the cows, fed and groomed the horses, and fed scratch to the chickens and turkeys.

And we did not do any of it out of dedication to the farm. It was done out of fear. Because if we did not listen, if we were not respectful, we had our actions corrected by being whipped by my dad with a rope provided by my grandfather. As a kid, it was a long, hard, and painful way to spend a summer. But for my father, it was productive.

When we were in Mexico, I thought about Alma all the time, but phone calls from Mexico to the states were almost impossible. But anytime I had money, I would get to a phone booth to call her. It made summers very long, but that made those phone calls so important.

It was hard work at my grandfather's farm, but there was one fun aspect of it. Did you know that Mexican people don't name horses like Americans do? They don't. They might name a cat or a dog, but never a horse. They are just a "horse," and there was this beautiful horse on the farm—an Alazan (chestnut) horse, the one I learned to ride on.

I was initially afraid of this horse. It was so big and strong, and I was so small and weak, but like I said, he was a good horse. Now, when learning to ride, you have to time your body with the horse's gallop and move accordingly; that was the first thing I learned, and it was also self-serving because by doing that, you lower the chance of being thrown off and getting hurt. My brother taught me that.

One day, we had some time off from the fields, and my brother wanted to go to our aunt's house. It wasn't a far walk, but my stubborn ass brother insisted we take the horse, but there was a problem—there was only one horse and two of us.

"Get on," my brother said. "Behind me."

"No," I said. "I'll walk."

He would not shut up, so I jumped up on the horse behind my brother and we rode. All was good until we got close to my aunt's house, and we had to pass through some narrow irrigation channels. We could not walk through them, so we slowly rode the horse, which was like walking a tightrope on the narrow strips of ground. We were almost through when one of the horse's hind legs slipped, and I fell off, landing straight on my back. That shook me, but I thought I was good, except that when I sat up to catch my breath, the frightened horse kicked, and in what seemed like slow motion, I saw his powerful hind legs zoom right by just enough past my head. I later reflected on this incident. Today, I can still see this in my mind, the slow-motion replay of those hooves moving toward my head. Had they connected, I might not be here.

I was so angry at my brother for wanting me to ride with him and angry at myself for agreeing. Once I began to realize how lucky I was, gratitude replaced anger.

Almost being kicked in the head by a horse could be one of the most dangerous things that can happen. But it wasn't. On another day, our cousins who lived there invited us kids to go hunting with them. I thought, cool, a break from the fields. We took a .22 caliber rifle and headed out looking for quail or deer or anything we could find. We didn't have any luck, so we headed back home. As we were walking back, a cousin spotted something.

"Look!" he shouted. And we all saw what he was pointing at—an iguana, just chilling on a tree branch. Now in Mexico, an iguana is prized, it is great eating, plus locals believe it has both medicinal and aphrodisiac properties. So bringing back an iguana would have made this a very productive day.

My cousin shot at the iguana. He missed. My other cousin tried. Miss. I tried, my cousins tried again—nothing. We were all such terrible shots that we couldn't hit that iguana. With no luck, we started to walk back home.

"One more shot," my cousin said, raising the butt of the rifle to his shoulder and taking aim. As he was about to shoot, my cousin and I were standing at a 90-degree angle from where he stood.
My cousin pulled the trigger, and the next thing I heard was this "FLING!" My cousin and I dove in opposite directions. The bullet ricocheted and flew inches between me and my cousin's head!
On the walk back home, I kept thinking about how lucky I was. Not to mention, we were three hours from the closest hospital.

Although all the kids were always looking for ways to find entertainment, the adults were no different. I remember my dad and uncles would have us little kids box each other while they drank and probably bet on who would win. This happened in my Tio Tomas's garage. They would put the boxing gloves on us and tell us to try and knock each other out.

I didn't like that part and hated hitting my cousins ... and hated being hit by them even more. Still, we obeyed.
Looking back, I remember having dizzy spells and the feeling of being pulled into the ground when I slept. It was an odd feeling that would come on quickly. I never knew if that was just a phase or something brought on by all the punches I took to the head.

Back in the States, my dad was working at a reputable business called Astro Arc. After 10 years or so, he wanted to open his own business. He and his brother created CATALAN MACHINE SHOP. This was a place where many family members learned the trade of machining. My dad and my uncle started with two machines and were doing well. But before they could grow the business, my uncle fell ill with terminal cancer. So what my dad had hoped would be a business with his brother became a business with his sons.

I began working at my dad's shop when I was around twelve years old and my brother was thirteen. My dad had us clean up the shop and, little by little, taught us how to use some of the less dangerous machines. My brother was good at math and really took an interest in machining more than anything, and he became my dad's right hand. I did the best I could.

The machines in the shop were all manual. With these machines, you had to actually use your hands to cut and drill—we did not get into CNC (automated) machines until the year 2000.

We had a couple small accidents at the shop, but nothing major. A cut finger here and a cut finger there, some worse than others, including a time I almost sawed my finger off on a vertical bandsaw, but we got by.

What's funny is that as I am writing this, I remember thinking of something I learned later on called Maslow's Hierarchy of Needs. These needs are shaped like a pyramid, and at the bottom of the pyramid, you have your physiological needs—breathing, food, water, shelter. On top of that, you have your safety and security needs—health, employment, property. Then comes the love and belonging need—friendship, family, intimacy. Then the self-esteem needs—confidence, achievement, the respect of others. And on the very top is the self-actualization needs—morality, creativity, and acceptance.

I think about that pyramid as I look back on my childhood and my relationship with my father. I see how scared I was as a kid. And because my dad was not the lovable type, I could not go to him for affection or self-assurance. My dad wasn't good at that; his expertise was in insults, reminding me of what a pendejo—dumbass—I was.

There was also the fact that my dad would make me feel like I was not a part of the family and that he always preferred my older brother. My brother was named after my dad, and he trusted him more, he was paid more at the shop, and even received a couple of cars, so I know I wasn't crazy thinking this.

I'm sorting through all of this as I write, not trying to establish blame, just trying to gather all the pieces together and understand all that came next. I have to agree with Maslow and his Hierarchy of Needs.

Incredibly and weirdly, I didn't realize that until I had to fight for my life in a murder case. But we're not at that part of the story yet. We're just getting to the first car I stole.

I never got hurt stealing cars, which is lucky because it's stupid and dangerous. One time, I was driving a stolen car around my high school, and I drove around twice before the police saw me, turned on their sirens, and chased me. I tried to get away for a little while, then realized I couldn't. So I stopped the car in the middle of traffic and ran through the backyards of nearby houses, jumping over fences and doing anything I could to get away.

Within five minutes, an LAPD helicopter was flying overhead, and I knew I had nowhere to go. I was about to hop into another backyard when I heard, "FREEZE!" With that order, I turned around, only to find myself staring at the barrel of a gun.

I was taken to the Van Nuys Police station to get booked, only to be released because I was a minor. Now, one might think that the police helicopter chase would be the part I'd remember the most. Nope. Here's what I remember.

When I was arrested, I'll never forget the LAPD cop who booked me. He was kind, talking to me about doing good, about doing bad, and what the difference was. He talked to me about Jesus Christ and how I should make my parents proud. I remember all of that. I remember him.

Of course, I didn't listen to him. I didn't take his advice and didn't make those changes until years later. But I'll never forget that man.

This same officer would later be involved in the infamous Bank of America North Hollywood shootout. He was shot and then he retired. And I like that he's still out there somewhere enjoying his retirement years.

I didn't go to jail for that first car theft.

Now, I had tried alcohol and marijuana, sure. I didn't really like alcohol, but I did like marijuana because it made me laugh. It wasn't long before I developed a taste for it, which required money. So I started tagging along with my brother on his adventures, which included breaking into cars and selling the parts—this was his side hustle, his part-time job.

One night, we were driving around when we spotted a beautiful Buick Regal, which was one of the more popular cars at the time. We pulled over and quickly broke into the car. What we didn't know was that a neighbor sitting on his porch was watching us the whole time. Of course, he called the cops, and about five to ten minutes after we left, what looked like the entire police department, helicopter and all, was after us. You would have thought we had just robbed a bank.

When the police saw my THUG LIFE t-shirt, they asked me if I was the one in charge. At the time I was sixteen years old definitely not a criminal mastermind. I spent two weeks in jail before I was released on probation.

My brother and I managed to stay out of trouble after that—that is, until we were introduced to forgery. A couple of my older cousins told us how easy it was to forge checks, so we did. Since we knew where our dad kept his business checkbook, we made some quick cash. Somehow, we didn't think of the fact that we were actually stealing from our father. To me, it was free money; I'm shaking my damn head as I think about it. I got away with it the first two times, but I got caught and arrested on my third try. They called my dad and then alerted the police. I didn't run this time. Instead, I waited for them.

I was put in jail for 30 days and then released on house arrest. If anything, I thought it was cool to go to school and show off the electronic device around my ankle. The conditions of the house arrest were that I could only go to school and work part-time with my dad. For the most part, I did rather well and followed the rules for the duration of the three months I was on house arrest. It was the weekends when it really bothered me that I couldn't go anywhere.

When the day came to go to court to remove the device, the judge said I needed more time and added 30 more days. I was so mad that when I got home, I called Alma.

"Let's go eat," I said.

"Eat?" she answered. "You mean at your house?"

"No, let's go out to eat, I'm sick of this."

So we left.

My dad, who always obeyed the law, drove me to Juvenile Hall in Sylmar, CA. and turned me in. I was so angry at him for that. But later, my mother told me that he cried the whole way home after doing it. While I was angry, I never held the fact that he turned me in against him because I knew I was in the wrong.

When it was time to go to court, I expected to be released under house arrest, again—so much that I probably seemed cocky when I stood in front of the judge.

He looked at me, and to my surprise, he didn't say anything about house arrest. He said I was a menace to society.

He sentenced me to a minimum of six months and a maximum of one year in juvenile camp.

I was numb. I tried to act tough, as if it didn't bother me. But it did. I got to speak to my mother in the visiting booth, and she was so upset—not at the judge, but at me.

Her face was beyond red the whole time she screamed at me. But I was in tough guy mode, and I just let her scream.

After that, I was escorted back to the holding tank, where I sat down with the rest of the inmates. Suddenly, a probation officer entered, looking just as angry as my mother.

"Whose mom just left?" he screamed.

I didn't pay any attention because there were a lot of moms out there. It could have been anyone's mom. When he didn't get an answer, he yelled again.

"Whose mom just left?" Wondering if he was talking about my mom, I hesitantly raised my hand. He could've been talking about my mom—I wasn't sure.

The officer yelled at me to come to the door where he stood. "Look!" he ordered, pointing at my mother. "Look what you did to her!"

I did look. And I saw my mother, crying and falling apart as she made her way toward the exit. She was a wreck. She was broken. I saw what I did to her.

Just like that, my tough guy persona was gone. When I got back to my seat, I couldn't hold it in anymore, and I put my head down and started crying.

After being released from camp six months later, I promised myself that I would never go back to jail.

I broke that promise. It just wasn't my fault.

So two down the splitter has done the job again for Reynolds, and here is Cesar Izturis. Fastball outside, ball one. One and 0. 2-1 Atlanta. We're in the bottom of the second inning with two outs. Reynolds comes back and misses high again, ball two, two and 0. Izturis is really doing a super job. He has a little four game hitting streak, but for two weeks, he's hit better than .360, and he has his average up to .264. But this time he fouls one away. Izturis has done a remarkable job of hitting left handed. He couldn't buy a base hit last year, and yet he kept saying 'I can do it; I can do it'. Well, right now he's hitting .255 left handed, and eleven of his twelve RBI's have come as a left-handed batter. Alex Cora has complemented him perfectly as he has turned himself around. And the two-one pitch groundball he chased a splitter almost in the dirt. And that'll be that as Marcus Giles throws him out. So Nomo will have to go back to pitching, and at the end of two, it's 2-1 Braves.

Vin Scully, Dodger's Stadium, May 12, 2003

CHAPTER THREE

LAKERS VS TIMBERWOLVES

*A*nd the batter is now Gary Sheffield, and here we go again. Sheffield hitting .500 against Hideo Nomo. Not only single driving in a run and for good measures stole second base. So Sheffield's at the plate. Gary Sheffield when he talks about his dad, he said his father was a construction worker on boats. Dived under the water, fixed the boats that you see in the movies. Gary wiggling that bat as always. Nomo delivers off speed for a strike, and the count 0 and 1. Gary got to wiggling the bat in 1988 in the minor leagues; it was an attempt to keep his hands back. He takes low and inside, and the count is one ball and one strike. Gary's also said he'd like to play baseball till he's at least forty. When Sheffield was with the Dodgers, he wore ten, but that's Chipper Jones number. So when Gary moved to Atlanta, he put on number eleven. Nomo delivers and that's low, and the count's two balls and one strike. When Gary Sheffield got out of high school into the minor leagues, he was way too quick, hitting a lot of balls foul, a lot of foul homeruns, so to slow himself down, he got to wiggling.

Vin Scully, Dodger's Stadium, May 12, 2003

The juvenile camp I was sent to was called Louis Routhe. Although I'd heard stories of the gang violence there, I didn't really know what to expect. The one thing I did know was that I could not show weakness. Thankfully, being seventeen and thinking I was a tough guy, I was good at acting tough.

I'm not sure why but being in jail for the first time reminded me of when my parents sent me to live with my godparents for a year. Those feelings of abandonment came on when I first entered camp, but I had to push them aside and put up a solid defense, because, really, I expected the worst.

When I entered camp, I was challenged by some of the inmates. I got in fights, I gave some, and took some, but I held my ground. The rules were everywhere, all monitored by the probation officers. For the most part, a few officers were cool, but most were not, and if there were official rules against officers touching inmates, that memo never got out.

And I did see some officers put their hands on inmates. One time, a kid asked to use the restroom. He used the urinal and when he was going to walk back, he decided to sit on the toilet. The probation officer saw this, and when he was walking back, the officer grabbed the kid's head and slammed him into the wall.

The first two weeks at Louis Routhe were a grueling boot camp style training. In the blazing sun, we carried fifty pounds of equipment up and down hills. We either completed the training, or we were shipped out. The day after surviving those first two weeks, we were required to shave off any facial hair to begin our actual stay. I have never been able to grow a beard, so I just had to get rid of my mustache.

I hated every minute of it. Besides having to watch my back, we were told when to eat, when to sleep, and when to shower. The schedule was constant--up at 6:00 a.m., breakfast at 7:00 a.m. Then the day consisted of a series of drills where we needed to get all the equipment ready to go and simulate fighting wildfires. Then it was lights out at 9:00 p.m. and rinse and repeat.

Like I said, most of the probation officers were not nice people. I know they had to make the experience a horrible one, not a pleasurable one. But there was one of them that was cool as hell, and I'll never forget him.

One day, this officer invited me and another inmate into his vehicle. Suddenly, we were riding out of camp. I looked at the other inmate, then the driver, then back, trying to figure out what was going on. But nobody said anything, and we just kept driving. Then I started to recognize that we were in my neighborhood. And before I knew it, we were in the parking lot of my dad's machine shop.

"Let's go say hi," the probation officer said, turning the vehicle off. So, we got out of the vehicle and followed him inside.

When my dad saw me, he thought I had escaped. My dad was told to drive quickly over to 7-11, where he bought Big Bites and Big Gulps for me and Q—that was the other kid's nickname.

We sat in my dad's shop, eating junk food, and not worried about anything at all.

I've never told that story before, but that day meant a lot to me.

I was so happy when the day finally came for me to go home. A total of three kids, myself included, were getting ready to be driven over to Sylmar Juvenile Court, which is where we would be released to your parents. As we were waiting in the main office for the van to arrive, the receptionist called me and the other two kids over to his desk. Then he opened a drawer and pulled out a book about the meaning of names.

He looked at us and said, "I'm going to tell you boys what your name means." I was surprised that he was even talking to us, but even more so that he was going to tell us what our names meant. He read the two first kids names as I waited. As soon as he was done, he looked at me and said, "Juan translated in English is John." Then, he proceeded to scroll through his book until he found my name. Pointing on a page, he read, "John means … whenever you find yourself in trouble, God will be with you." I felt those words in my soul, and I have never forgotten them.

Finding out that I was going to be a father was one of the happiest moments of my life. I told my family and friends. I told the world. We went shopping for the baby, we picked out a name, we planned, and we talked. It was an amazing time; not just for Alma and me, but also for my mom and Alma's mom since this would be the first grandchild for both of them. There would be sixteen grandchildren to follow—they didn't know that yet —but our child would be the first.

Alma began her prenatal care and had many checkups. At one of them, they saw something they wanted to check.

"What is it?" Alma asked.

"We need to do a test because there is a high probability that your child could be born with Down syndrome," the doctor said.

"What kind of test?" Alma asked.

The doctor explained that she needed an amniocentesis test, which involves inserting a needle into the mother's stomach to collect amniotic fluid to see if there were any signs that the baby might have Down syndrome. However, the test itself poses a risk because it could cause a miscarriage.

"A miscarriage?" Alma asked.

"There's a very low chance the test will do that," said the doctor. "One in 400. But if we determine the child has Down syndrome, then there is still time to abort."

Alma was uncontrollably distraught. We went to church, and we prayed. In the end, we decided to choose faith and believe that whatever God had planned for us was His will and we would accept it. When we went back to the doctor, we told him our decision.

One in 400 was small, but it was still a chance of a miscarriage, and we didn't want to take that chance. Instead, we would have faith in whatever God had planned for us.

And on December 27, 1997. Mellisa Marie Catalan was born. She was perfect. She still is.

When I finally got to hold my daughter for the first time, I fell in love with her instantly.

"You know what?" I told baby Melissa, walking her around the hospital room. "I am going to be the best dad possible to you."

When I left the hospital that day, I drove right to the church and got on my knees once again. "Thank you, God," I cried. "Thank you."

When Alma became pregnant for the second time, a year and a half later, it was unexpected. We were both now 21 years of age. So even though we were biologically in our twenties, we were forced to grow up faster. After all, I was still trying to understand what it meant to be a father the first time when I found out that I was going to be a father for the second time.

That's the good news. The bad news is that I didn't have a real job or a place of my own. I also didn't have a plan for the future. Alma saw this.

"You need to be more responsible," she said. "It's not just you anymore; you have me, and soon you'll have two daughters."

Alma's pregnancy with Mariah was different than when she carried Melissa. Melissa was quiet. Mariah was rowdy. In fact, Mariah moved around so much that when Alma went into labor, Mariah had gotten the umbilical cord wrapped around her neck. This would require an emergency c-section.

Thirty-six hours later, on June 7, 1999, Mariah Elizabeth Catalan was born. She was chubby and as white as bread. When I heard Mariah's first cry, it was the most beautiful sound I had ever heard in my life.

Not having a job or a house, one thing I could do was stay out of trouble. And one way to do that was to work at my dad's machine shop. It was honest, it was steady, and I had my dad there to remind me that I was now a father.

"You can't be acting like that anymore," he said.

"I know."
"
You're a father now."

"I know, I know."

"You now have others to think about besides yourself."
And I did know—he was right. I also knew that I wanted my daughters' childhoods to be better than mine.

It's very hard to explain what it's like to have kids at a young age, especially to those parents who waited to have children. At a time when I would have typically been planning my own future, I was trying to think about my daughters' future.

You sort of put yourself on hold, and it causes a great deal of confusion and stress.

But for some weird reason, I have always preferred the more interesting road, rather than the easy road. Looking back, it seems like I have done everything backwards—including college, which we'll get to. I thank God that He gave me a warrior's spirit because I don't know how much harder this life would be without one.

Now that I had two daughters, I knew I wanted to be a part of their lives, so I began to distance myself from the gang life. I still had some close friends who were in gangs, but besides them, I left that life and was staying out of trouble.

The problem was that even though I didn't do anything to get myself in trouble, it came, anyway.

And this trouble was the worst kind.

In November of 2022, my brother was involved in a very serious situation, and neither one of us knew that our lives were about to change forever.

It was the Sunday after Thanksgiving, December 1, 2002. I was getting ready to settle in and watch the Lakers, who were playing the Timberwolves. The TV was on, and I was relaxed.

Until—

BAM – BAM – BAM.

I looked to the door and thought, You've got to be kidding me, as I put my drink down. Who is going to fuck up me watching this game? Although I was pissed, I didn't feel that way for very long because right after the pounding came a voice behind the door.

"LAPD! OPEN UP!"

I froze.

I could only think of one reason why the police might be here. I was pretty sure that my brother, Mario, had drugs in the house—probably a lot of them. And I would need to find them and get rid of them before—.

The door flew open, revealing a dozen LAPD officers wearing bulletproof vests.

"LAPD," the one in front screamed. "We have a warrant to search this property."

The police entered and ordered us all sit in the living room.

"Is Mario Catalan your son?" the man asked my father.

"Yes."

"He's been arrested," the policeman said.

"Arrested?" my dad asked. "For what?"

The policeman waved the other officers in. "As an accessory to murder." Handing a paper to my father, he continued. "And this warrant gives us the right to look for the murder weapon."

As we all sat there—my father, my mother, my little sisters, and me—I wasn't sure what to do next. It didn't take the police long to find Mario's drugs. First, they found several pounds of marijuana, which they sat on the coffee table in front of us. Then they left to look for more. When they returned, they placed a bag of methamphetamine next to it.

The officer picked up the bag of pot, "This," he said, "I can ignore." He placed the bag down and picked up the meth. "But this," he smiled, "I can't.

The cop allowed a few moments to build and then asked the loaded question, "So whose is this?"
Looking at him, then my father, I knew I had a choice to make. Taking a deep breath, I answered.

"It's mine," I said.

The officer looked at me in a way that told me he knew the drugs weren't mine.

"Cuff him," he said.

They did.

A few hours later, I was taken to the police station and charged with possession of a controlled substance with intent to distribute.
It was a terrible night in more ways than one: to make matters worse, the Timberwolves beat the Lakers 110 to 107.

And the batter will be Paul LoDuca. The Braves have not only won twenty-one of the last twenty-five games they've played, they have even won nine of the last ten games they've played on the road. You probably know because it's been written up a lot. The Braves have won sixty-nine consecutive games in which John Smoltz has appeared; that's a major league record. So Bobby has a lot of talent, and he knows how to use it, which is more important. Now the pitch to LoDuca, a strike, and tomorrow night Atlanta sends Russ Ortiz to the mound. Ortiz has won his last four starts at Dodger Stadium; however, Wednesday night Greg Maddux is winless in his last four starts at Dodger Stadium. So Kevin Brown will try to keep that record perfect Wednesday night. Here's the strike one pitch to LoDuca, that's low, and the count one ball one strike. LoDuca drove a line drive down the right field line in the first inning, and Gary Sheffield who was shaded a wee bit over that way made a fine one-hand running catch. One and one to LoDuca.

Vin Scully, Dodger's Stadium, May 12, 2003

CHAPTER FOUR

MARTHA

S *o, Nomo struck out Andruw Jones upstairs, and now he puts Lopez away upstairs, and the batter will be Vinny Castilla. When Vinny was in high school in Mexico, he was a big soccer player and squash, but his father was a baseball player and as Vinny said, "You do what your dad does." So, he turned to another sport. Ball one. Castilla idolized Ozzie Smith and, of course, anybody who ever saw Ozzie play could understand that. His father was a teacher educating elementary kids by day and high school students at night. One and one. And he has a brother who works for the government, and once Vinny started to make some money, he bought his parents a new home and two cars. So, a generous son. Like Javy Lopez, when he signed on, he didn't speak any English at all, and he was drafted by Colorado in the expansion draft in 1992 from Atlanta, and he set the league on fire for a couple of years. Remember what a homerun hitter Vinny Castilla was? We mentioned it earlier, 32 then back to back years of 40, then 46, 33. So the Dodgers still have to be very careful with him. One and one.*

Vin Scully, Dodger's Stadium, May 12, 2003

I was arrested and booked and spent two days at the police station waiting for my court date. Inside was also my brother, Mario, who was there on this new murder charge, and we ended up in the same holding tank. I was so angry at my brother, I just wanted out.

"I took the blame for you, asshole," I said.

Mario just stared at me.

When I met with the public defender, his news was simple. "You're looking at five years," he told me.

"What? But the drugs weren't mine."

"Are you willing to state that in court?"

I looked away. The next day I faced the judge. "How do you plead?" the judge asked.

"Not guilty," the public defender stated. My bail was set at $50,000, which we didn't have, so I was sent on my first trip to County.

County refers to the Men's Central Jail, where I spent two days until being transferred to the Pitchess Detention Center, better known as "Wayside." They ran this facility as close to a prison as you could get without actually being called one.

After two weeks at Wayside, I had my next court date. As we stood in front of the judge, my public defender spoke.

"I would ask the court that Mr. Catalan be released on his own recognizance, your honor." "Your honor," the Deputy District Attorney objected. "Mr. Catalan is a threat to society. He should remain incarcerated until the trial."

Now, when a judge is silent, especially when considering whether you are leaving this building, it seems to take forever. The judge sat quiet, deep in thought, then she looked at me.

"I'm going to take a chance on you, Mr. Catalan," she said. "Don't disappoint me."

The public defender seemed shocked that I was being let out on O.R. At first, I didn't understand what was going on. But then it hit me. I was going home. At least for now.

Sure, I had a drug charge and a possible prison sentence hanging over my head. But I was also with my family for Christmas, which was the most important.

I had to go back to court a few times on the drug charge, but Mario had an accessory to murder charge that carried a life sentence or, at best, a million-dollar bail.

I met with my public defender regularly.

"We're working on it," was his standard response. He had little to report, because without me stating that the drugs were my brother's, we both knew there was little to go on.

"You can always plead to a lesser charge," he informed me. But this meant accepting a prison sentence for something I didn't do.

But as much trouble as I was in, my brother, Mario, was in far worse. And there was no way that he had any chance with a public defender. He needed a high profile—and expensive—criminal lawyer.

"I want Alex Kessel," Mario told my father.

Mario knew of this guy only because he had heard about him getting some people off from our neck of the woods.

My dad didn't like the idea of spending that kind of money on an attorney, but he liked the idea of his oldest son getting a prison sentence of life even less.

So my dad and I went to meet Alex Kessel.

"I've had much tougher cases," Kessel said, putting his hands behind his head and leaning back in his chair.
And he painted a good picture. A hopeful picture. Unfortunately, it was also a $47,000 picture.

"That's a lot of money," my dad replied.

"It is," Kessel leaned forward and looked at the papers on his desk. "But it is a life sentence your son is looking at.'

Dad took out a loan on his house and paid Kessel the $47,000.

Kessel took the case and quickly realized that his first hurdle was that Mario's case was tied to his co-defendant's case. That did not help Mario at all. Kessel tried to get the two cases separated but couldn't. So, Mario would be tried in with the larger case. This would make it even more difficult for Mario.

***It was now around March, and I had to make a decision whether to stick with my public defender or hire an attorney, as well. I looked around at some different lawyers and even met with one or two, but I never felt sure or that any of them even cared. None of them clicked, but one did say something that stuck with me.

"You know," he said, "I don't know if it's how you Hispanics are raised, but you guys will do anything to protect your family. It is a very noble thing, and I admire that." I took it as a compliment, but it got me thinking.

My cousin, Carlos, worked as a filing clerk at a law office. On different family occasions, he would brag about a bad ass lawyer. The only thing was no one needed a lawyer at the time.

"If you guys ever need a lawyer, Todd Melnik is your guy."

Never in a million years did I imagine that I would be the one who did.

Todd asked me to meet him at the Van Nuys Courthouse. When I walked into the courtroom where he was, he looked at me and gave me the biggest Kool-Aid smile. For some reason, I knew right then that he was the one. What I did not know was that Todd would protect me as much as he could—as much as anyone could.

Todd and I made a deal for him to represent me in the drug charge, and I left with not only a sense of relief, but a really good feeling about Todd.

Now that I had retained Todd, I felt my family could concentrate on my brother's case. It was around April 2003, and with his preliminary hearing in a few weeks, Mario was constantly calling the house.

"I need everyone there," my brother said.

"Why?"

"Because judges look at the family, they want to see family that supports them and will be there for them."
Unfortunately, with my dad working all the time, and my mom's anxiety, this family presence fell on my shoulders.

"Okay," I said. "I'll be there for you."

I asked Alma, my sister, and my good friend, Ruben, to come along with me. With me, that meant a family of four would be sitting behind my brother.

When we all stepped into the courtroom, the tension was undeniable. All eyes turned to us as we took our seats, and I saw, for the first time, Martha Puebla—who will be critical to this story later on. This would be the only time I saw Martha, as she was murdered less than a month later.

We took our seats, and my brother's preliminary hearing began.

I noticed that there were many looks back at us. Then whispers. Then discussions. Then a uniformed LAPD officer walked up to us.

"Could you step outside in the hall for a minute, please," he requested in a soft but authoritarian tone.

"Me?" I asked, confused.

"All of you," he pointed to the four of us. "Please follow me out to the hall."

We did.

The officer was joined by another officer, and they asked to see our identification. They wrote down everything and then stated that we would need to leave the courtroom.

"Leave? Why?" I asked.

"The Deputy District Attorney, feels that you are here to intimidate the witness."

I started to laugh, then realized that he was serious. I had the officer look at the four of us, two average looking men and two young women.

"That's ridiculous," I said.

After some back and forth, we were allowed to go back into the courtroom.

When hearing was almost done, Martha Puebla took the stand. She was sworn in and began her testimony. Again, she had nothing to do with my brother's case and was a witness in his co-defendant's case. Just as she was finishing, attorney Kessel rose and stood behind my brother.

Placing his hands on my brother's shoulders, he asked, "Do you know this man, Mario Catalan?"

Martha looked at my brother and then back to the attorney.
"No," she said. "I do not."

Here's Shawn Green, then Fred McGriff and Brian Jordan. Ball one over his head. Braves 2, Dodgers 1, bottom of the fourth. It's 1-0 up north, the Giants leading Montreal. Giants might've scored a bunch in the fourth inning, Brad Wilkerson playing left field made a great diving rolling catch to take two runs away from the Giants, so it's still 1-0 San Francisco. AND A DRIVE TO CENTER, BACK GOES ANDRUW TO THE TRACK, TO THE WALL, REACHES UP AND MAKES THE CATCH! Andruw Jones goes back and picks it off like it's an apple on a tree, taking a homerun away from Shawn Green. He's the best out there, right at the wall reached up and picked it off. Andruw Jones says that when he was a little boy every single day in Curacao, his dad would take him down to the beach and hit balls up in the air. And at the beach in Curacao, the wind is always blowing, and he said it was much tougher to catch those pop flies that his father would hit on the beach than it is to even catch a ball like just now with Shawn Green.

May 12, 2003

CHAPTER FIVE

NO LIES DETECTED

2-1 Atlanta, top of the fifth inning. Rafael Furcal will lead it off, followed by Marcus Giles and then Gary Sheffield. Furcal always a threat to bunt, one ball and no strikes. His on base percentage fifth among National League leadoff men, and he's hitting .329. Two and 0 the count to Rafael. Youngest of four children and at 5' 10", he's become the big man in the family, strike. Two and one. He moved his parents from the Dominican to Atlanta in the middle of his rookie year, then when he made some money, he bought them a home in the Dominican, and they went back. Two and one. Interesting, too, when he was the National League Rookie of the Year, he was the first middle infielder to win the award since Steve Sax. And he was the first Dominican since Raul Mondesi. Popped in the air, foul off to the left, LoDuca over but that's out of play. One thing about Rafael Furcal, HBO ran a special report on him back in 2000. It stated that Furcal was three years older than he was listed, and Rafael was irritated and said his mom was sending his birth certificate from the Dominican. He said, "I'm the youngest of a family of five." He draws the walk. However, the true age ended up being just like HBO said, he was two years older than he had put down on paper.

Vin Scully, Dodger's Stadium, May 12, 2003

49

"I've got great news," my attorney, Todd Melnik, told me over the phone.

Yeah?" I answered enthusiastically. "I could use some."

"I know how I'm going to get you off this drug case. Can you come to my office?"

Todd didn't say, I think I've found something, or I may have an idea, nope. It was, I know what to do.

"Sure," I said, so excited I wanted to leave right then.

I couldn't wait to get to Todd's office, and when I did, Todd greeted me with his big Kool-Aid smile.

"So a gentleman will be here in about ten minutes," he said. "With a lie detector."

"Okay," I said, not sure where this was going.

"And you are going to state that these were your brother's drugs."

I blinked, looked around the room, and then back to Todd.

A knock came at the door, and Todd let in an older gentleman who was carrying a large case. The man shook my hand and began to set up the polygraph, while I sat there with a blank stare on my face.

"What's wrong?" Todd asked.

"I'm not doing that. I'm not taking that," I told him.

"What? Why not?"

"I would never tell on one of my friends, let alone my own brother."

Todd gave me a deep stare.

"That's the point," I told him. "Yes, they were Mario's drugs. I know it, you know it, my family knows it. But I am not going to rat him out. I'm in this mess because I wanted to protect him. I won't rat him out. You've got to find another way."

Todd took a second and made me slip the man a hundred dollars for his trouble.

Mothers' Day fell on Sunday, May 11th in 2003, and being the super considerate boyfriend I am, I got Alma Dodger tickets for a gift— yeah, I did that. It wasn't the first time, either. I bought four tickets to the Dodger's game against the Atlanta Braves, but strangely enough, Alma had no interest in going to the game.

Super weird.

"But it's Kevin Brown," I said, trying to sell it. "He should be in the Hall of Fame, playing against Greg Maddux!"

Alma didn't care.

The game was on the following Wednesday, May 14, and I began that week excited to know I was going to be at Wednesday's game.

One of our best customers back then was with a company called Arc Machines. The purchasing agent was named Cesar Castillo, and on Monday morning, Cesar called me.

"Hey, I have four tickets to the Dodgers game tonight. You interested?"

Cesar was often given tickets from vendors, so yeah, absolutely I would take them.

I asked Alma if she wanted to go to the game, but she didn't want to, so I called my cousin, Ruben, my friend, Miguel, and I was going to take my daughter, Melissa.

I picked everyone up around 6 p.m. and drove to the stadium. Thirty minutes before the first pitch, we walked in.

Now, I'm not sure how to explain the feeling I get when I walk into Dodger Stadium. It's almost magical, as if I'm supposed to be there. I tell people it's like my second home with all the time I've spent there.

We walked toward our seats, which were amazing by the way— Field level 29, third base side, row Vee, seats 1-4. We took our seats excited to watch the perennial powerhouse Atlanta Braves taking on one of the best pitchers the Dodgers had, Hideo Nomo.

The game started with both teams scoring a run each in the first inning. The Braves would add another in the top of the second inning and another in the top of the fifth inning. The Dodgers responded in the bottom of the fifth by adding a run to cut the lead to 3-2. The Braves came back and tacked on another run in the top of the sixth, but the Dodgers responded with one of their own in the bottom of the sixth. The score was now 4-3 Braves.

About that time, my daughter, Melissa, asked me for ice cream and candy. I really didn't want to miss the action, but I would rather miss some of the game earlier, rather than later in the game. I got up from our seats and went to the concession stands and bought Melissa what she wanted. When we headed back to our seats, we were completely surprised to see that our aisle was blocked off by TV cameras.

My first thought was how cool it was that cameras were on our aisle—maybe we would be caught on camera. I then tried to get back to our seats, hoping we could walk in front of the camera. But production assistant stopped me.

"Can you wait just a minute, please," he said. "We need to get this shot."

"No problem," I said.

As we looked on, an older gentleman kept walking up and down the aisle stairs. Then, out of the corner of my eye, I noticed this P.A. (as they're called) looking over at me and Melissa. After looking at us from head to toe, he did something very strange.

"Just go ahead," he said. I looked at him in disbelief, thinking, Wow!

How cool is this that we're going to be on camera! I took Melissa by the hand, and as soon as we started down the stairs, the gentleman they were filming began walking up the stairs. When he saw me, he threw his hands up in the air, obviously frustrated because we had cut him off. Oops!

I was hoping the P.A. didn't get fired for that, because that single act well, it altered my life.

We got back to our seats and watched the game … and, man, it was a good one. The Dodgers tied the game in the bottom of the seventh, and it was surely going to go down to the wire. All the while, the filming continued on our aisle.

And while keeping an eye on the game, I kept trying to figure who the man was who was walking up and down the stairs.

"They're filming Super Dave Osbourne," someone said from the row behind us.

Cool, I thought. I knew who that was.

The game entered the ninth inning with the score still tied 4-4. At the time, the Dodgers had the best closer in baseball, a player named Eric Gagne, who happened to have the nickname "Game Over," so there was no way that the Braves were going to score in the top of the ninth—at least that was my thought. I was thinking Gagne would shut them out in the ninth, and we would come up in the bottom of the ninth and win the game. I couldn't have been more wrong.

The Braves scored. Not once —but SEVEN times!

I looked over at my five-year-old daughter and told my cousin and friend that it was time to go. I was a huge believer in comebacks, but even I knew they wouldn't be coming back from seven runs. Everyone agreed, and we got up and headed toward the exit.

On the way out, we came across a stand selling baseball cards. Having loved baseball cards while growing up, I had taught my daughters about sports cards, so Melissa asked right away if we could buy some. We stopped and made our purchase, and as we were walking out of the stadium, Alma called me on my cell phone. She asked where we were, and I told her we were walking out of the stadium.

The time was just after 10 p.m. We all hopped in our Tahoe and started on our way home. Now, there are many horror stories about L.A. traffic, especially during a sporting event, but being born and growing up in L.A., I get to know the shortcuts, so I was able to get to and from Sun Valley in approximately 30 minutes. The plan was to drop off Miguel and then Ruben and then head back to Alma's house. Miguel only lived five blocks from my house on Case Avenue, and I got to his house around 10:40. I then drove south on Case Avenue toward what was Keswick Street.

After turning left toward Vineland Avenue, I dropped him off and then proceeded to Alma's house. When we got there, I opened the baseball cards with my daughters, and as we talked, we organized our cards. That was our night.

***

Life was normal for the next couple of weeks until Ruben showed up at the shop. I could tell something was wrong as soon as I saw him.

"What?" I asked. "What happened?"

Ruben handed me that day's Daily News and pointed to an article. "This—this is what happened."

I

"Murder witness is murdered" the headline read.

The article reported that a 16-year-old girl, Martha Puebla, was killed.

"Damn," I said. "But what does this have to do with us?"

"Don't you remember? They tried to kick us out of the courtroom that day, saying we were intimidating the witness. They took down our information and said we were trying to intimidate—her!"

Then—it hit me.

"Holy shit," I said.

"But they can't."

"Why not? It fits," Ruben stated.

I wasn't going to entertain the idea, so I let it go.

Fast forward to August 11, 2003. Alma and I had broken up. That night, I had the strangest dream I've ever had. In the dream, I was walking outside my house when all of a sudden what seemed to be aliens were everywhere. While they were trying to take me away, I resisted, but they kept coming. The whole time I was feverishly trying to escape.

Then, I woke up.

I felt incredibly weird, so I called Alma and asked if she would come over and spend the night.

Alma turned me down at first, but I asked again. She mentioned that Melissa and Mariah were already sleeping, and she was not going to leave them. Then she quickly changed her mind, saying that Mariah woke up, and she could leave Melissa with her mom and come over. I was a bit more at ease, but I still couldn't go back to sleep for a while.

When I woke up, I explained in detail to Alma. It wasn't until Alma dropped me off at work the next morning that everything happened.

As we pulled up to my dad's shop, I glanced at the passenger mirror and saw a mid-size SUV block us in from behind.

"Who the fuck is this?" I asked.

I opened the door quickly, thinking this was some kind of L.A. road rage, and the biker-looking driver of the other car got out at the same time. When I stepped out, I was surprised to find that I was staring at the barrel of a gun.

"GET ON THE GROUND," he screamed. "NOW!"

I froze. Because he looked like a biker and wasn't wearing a uniform, I didn't think he was a cop. Before I could obey, I found myself in a SWAT-style takedown. Seconds later, multiple cops were on top of me and my face was on the asphalt,

"What are you doing? I haven't done—."

One of them stuck a printout in front of my face, and I could see that it was my booking sheet from the drug charge. He looked at me, the sheet, then back to me.

"That's him," he said. "This is the guy."

"What are you doing?" I yelled. "What have I done?

But they didn't answer me. Instead, I was handcuffed. So was Alma.

Then my dad came out of the shop. "Dad!" I yelled. "Look what they're doing to me."

I was lying face down on the asphalt as the crowd around me began to grow with curious neighbors and friends. I heard someone crying and realized it was my four-year-old daughter, Mariah.

Motherfuckers.

"What are you guys doing?"

"The detectives want to talk to you."

"About—about what?

"The detectives will explain everything."

I was walked to the back of a squad car and driven to the North Hollywood Police Station. It occurred to me that they hadn't read me my rights, but I had bigger concerns right then to remind them.

I was put in a holding cell and found it unusual that I was alone. In my experience with the criminal justice system, you are never alone. The prison system is so crowded, so full, that being alone is a luxury that never occurs.

It was cold and quiet while I waited in my holding cell. I sat on the steel bench for a second or two and then I would get up and pace. If I was still, I could just hear some of the conversations going on in the station beyond the door. Just then, I heard the back door swing open.

"Who do we have back there?" a deep voice asked.

"Only a 187 suspect."

My heart dropped. Everyone who grew up around a neighborhood like mine knew what a 187 was. It's the penal code for murder.

"Please God," I whispered. "Let them be talking about someone else."

I waited for over six hours until they pulled me out. Then I was escorted to an interrogation room—you know the room you see in the movies, containing just a table, two or three chairs, and a big two-way mirror.

Two detectives walked in.

"My name is Detective Martin Pinner," one of them said. "And this is Detective Juan Rodriguez."

"Why am I here?" I asked.

"We'll get to that," said Pinner. "But we have some questions for you first."

They asked a couple of easy questions, some softball identification ones to try and establish some trust. I just wanted to know what the fuck was going on—then they dropped the bomb on me.

"You've been arrested for the murder of Martha Puebla."

I went numb as I tried to process what I had just heard. What?

The detectives asked a few questions after that, but it took me a few minutes to mentally snap back into it.

"It," I started, trying to clear my head. "It wasn't me."

"Sure, it was," Pinner said.

"No, no it wasn't. You've got the wrong person—you have the wrong person."

"No," Pinner leaned forward. "It was you. We have witnesses."

"Impossible," I said. "There's—no way."

Detective Pinner slid something called a six pack across the table. It is a collection of six separate mugshots, and my picture was one of them. There were comments handwritten on them, and my picture was circled. I leaned in to read was written.

This is the guy who I saw shoot my neighbor.

I looked up at them, then back to the paper, allowing my mind to catch up. Why would someone say I did this?

"Where were you on the night of May 12th, 2003?"

"When?" I couldn't take my eyes off the paper. "What night?"

"Monday, May 12th, 2003?"

"I don't—. That was three months ago; how would I know where I was?"

But they kept pressing me. "Admit it," they'd say. "Just admit it, and things will go easier."

"We know you killed her."

"Stop fucking saying that!" I screamed.

It continued like this for a solid twenty minutes. "We're here to help you," Pinner said. "If you confess, then we can recommend leniency to the judge."

"But I didn't do it!"

Rodriguez was silent most of this time and had a strange look on his face, so I thought maybe he was the one I could try to reason with.

He made a comment that still infuriates me to this day. I didn't know that they had raided Alma's house, and Alma told him that they had the wrong person. His response? "Well, help us find the right person," and then handed her his card.

What the fuck? So that means they weren't sure if I was guilty or not. What a fucking disappointment in our legal system.

"Por favor ayudeme yo no hice esto!" And Rodriguez then snapped out of it and joined his buddy.

"We know you did it," Rodriguez said. "Just admit it."

"Give me a lie detector test," I said. "I'll take it right now."

They refused. Why?

Then I told them what they had probably heard a thousand times from that very room.

"You two are making the biggest mistakes of your careers," I said.

But they just smiled.

They had probably heard that a thousand times, but there was one difference this time—that phrase came true.

While I was fingerprinted and booked, I continued my rant to anyone

I saw in a uniform.

"I didn't do this," I said. "You've got to believe me, I didn't."

Most of the officers just ignored me. But one female officer looked at me for a second and responded.

"Just pray," she said.

I was put in a holding cell again to await a court date to see a judge. Two days later, I had my court date and was pulled out to meet with a public defender.

"You are being booked for Capital Murder with special circumstances," he said with little emotion. "Which, if found guilty, you could be looking at the death penalty."

"Death penalty?" I asked, the words hanging in the air. "But I didn't do this."

"Well," he said, flipping through the file, "they have a witness, a Mr. Sam, who said that you did."

Mr. Sam? I thought.

The public defender and I went in to see the judge.

"How do you plead?" she asked.

"Not guilty."

I was led out of court and put back to the holding tank. That's when I noticed the TV cameras inside the courtroom and wondered what they were there for. It wasn't until I had a chance to speak to Alma that she told me that some family members had been watching me on the news.

***

As I waited for the Los Angeles Sheriff Department bus, the officers shackled my hands to my waist, and they shackled my feet together. It was then that I realized that the shit had gotten real. When I boarded the bus, I was isolated in a single cage. I was considered to be the worst of the worst.

During the ride over to Men's Central Jail, better known as The County—which was ranked as one of the ten worst jails/prisons in the country—my mind was spinning.

Scenes of my life—both the good and the bad—played through my mind as I looked out onto the streets of L.A. I had to wonder if this was it—would I be locked up forever … or worse?

When we arrived, I was taken to processing to be interviewed by another deputy. Was I a gang member? Do I have enemies? Do I fear for my life? Do I have suicidal thoughts?

When the inquisition was over, they gave me a white bracelet with my name and booking number on it. Then the officer asked me to give him my hand.

"My what?" I asked, confused.

"Your hand, give me your hand."

With a black Sharpie, he took my hand and wrote the number 187 on it.

When I returned to my seat, other inmates moved away and didn't make eye contact. Only one spoke. Tattooed from head to toe, he looked at my hand and said,

"They don't want you to go home."

I was taken to the 2000 floor, which was for the most part "cracking," like they say in the streets. Before I could be placed in a cell, I was instructed to shower in the worst sanitary conditions I'd ever seen. I will spare you the details, because, believe me, you don't want to know. From there, I was taken to dorm that was designed for 50 inmates. At that time, it housed more than 100.

I was greeted by the raza, the Hispanics, and given a rundown on the house rules. From the moment I arrived, that 187 stamped on my hand made inmates think twice about talking to me. My fear was that something bad would happen because of it. After all, I was being accused of killing a 16-year-old girl who happened to be pregnant. In jail, there are some crimes that are not tolerated, such as snitching, rape, and any crimes against kids. And here I was, accused of murdering a young girl.

On that first day, a "trustee,"—inmates who help around the jail with cleaning and running errands—came to our dorm and told the homies that he had information about someone who was "no good."

From what I overheard, it was regarding a "piece of shit" inmate. The trustee said he would share the information after dinner that night. I was certain he was talking about me. As the hours passed, I was sure that if the trustee did as he promised, my life would be over. And for something I didn't do.

Dinner came, and I couldn't eat.

In another act of divine intervention, we heard a commotion just as we were leaving the chow room. We all looked out the dorm, only to see that trustee pinned to a wall by a sheriff deputy who had his elbow to the trustee's neck! The trustee was taken to the hole before he had a chance to tell the other inmates anything! I survived day one.

On the second day, I called my family to see what new information they had. During our conversation, I mentioned the date of the murder to Alma, and she recalled that it was around Mother's Day weekend.

"Weren't you at the Dodgers game that day?" she asked.

She was right. I was so excited that I had Alma make a three-way call right then to Todd, who happened to be playing golf in Canada. Since I was just wrapping my head around this murder charge, I still had not called him.

"Todd?"

"Hey Juan, how are—?"

"You are not going to believe this, but I was arrested for murder."

"WHAT!" Todd replied in disbelief.

After digesting the news for a moment, Todd was all business. He told me he would be back the next Monday and ordered me not to talk to anyone about my case.

On the third day, deputies called me out of the dorm and told me to roll up my belongings because I was being moved. Along the way, they informed me that I was being placed in solitary confinement, also known as High Power.
"Why am I being put in there?" I asked.

The deputy ignored me and didn't answer my question until they exchanged my white bracelet with a blue bracelet that had K-2 written on it.

"Confused, I asked the deputy what K-2 meant.

"Because you fear for your life," he explained.

What the fuck, I thought. I was put in a one-man cell that was among what seemed to be a long row of cells. The inmate to my left had just come in from Pelican Bay, which had a reputation for being one of the most dangerous prisons in California. When this inmate saw my bracelet, he asked me if my crime had anything to do with kids. His question bothered me, so I denied it.

"Nah, man." But I knew I was being accused of killing a 16-year-old girl.

Atlanta 3-1 over the Dodgers, bottom of the fifth inning. Mike Kincade, Adrain Beltre, and Cesar Izturis against Shane Reynolds, who lived a very fortunate life in the fourth inning. Green lost a possible homerun on a leaping one-hand catch by Andruw Jones. Sheffield speared a line drive going into the right field wall, AND A HIGH TOWERING DRIVE INTO DEEP LEFT CENTERFIELD. THEY CAN'T CATCH THAT ONE! And that makes it 3-2 Atlanta. So Mike Kincade hits his second homerun, his fourth RBI that gets them a little closer, and boy he got all of that thing. Fastball up and he just muscled it into the bleachers. So a leadoff homerun seems to wake up everybody as Kincade hits it out, and now here's Beltre.

Vin Scully, Dodger's Stadium, May 12, 2003

CHAPTER SIX

GLASS WALL

O *n this day in Dodger history back in 1956, a night game at Ebbets*
field with the New York Giants and pitching for the Brooklyn Dodgers
right hander Carl Erskine. Erskine pitched a no-hitter, beat the Giants three to
nothing and two big defensive plays saved his bacon. Jackie Robinson playing
third base took an extra base hit away from Willie Mays. Carl Furillo went into
deep right centerfield to backhand a ball hit by Daryl Spencer. Carl Erskine two
no-hitters, pitched one against the Cubs in 1952. And talking about pitching,
let's go back to this one. 3-2 in favor of Atlanta and Nomo ready to make pitch
number 99 as he begins the sixth inning with Javy Lopez. Strike. Javy Lopez
flied to center, struck out, oh for two. Trying to get the inside corner but he
missed, one ball and one strike. Lopez first came up to the Braves in 1992 and,
of course, the Braves dominated the 90's. Ball two, two and one. So Nomo has
now made a hundred and one pitches. Odalis Perez, remember the game he
pitched; he made a hundred and thirty-two. Ho ho, he still got some stuff in the
tank. Two and two the count. Javy Lopez hit a very big homerun, but he hit in
the Puerto Rican winter league. Not with that swing. He hit a homerun to beat
the Cuban national team. The Cuban team had won a hundred and one games
so he became the biggest man in Latin America.

Vin Scully, Dodger's Stadium, May 12, 2003

I was locked in solitary confinement, which is a 7' x 9' cell. And no, that's not a typo—7 feet—by 9 feet.

To give you some perspective of the size of this cell, a standard municipal parking spot is 16' X 9'. That means a parking spot would be almost the same size as two solitary confinement cells. A better comparison would be the average-sized throw rug, which would be around 9' X 12'.

As I looked forward from my cell, I could see the bars of the cell door and my reflection in the mirror behind it. So for 23 hours a day, I could pace, try to sleep, or look at myself. I could hear the sheriffs and deputies outside, and they could see into my cell through the two-way mirror, but I could not see them. I was totally isolated from the world inside that tiny box, and the mirror made it seem even smaller—like a box within a box.

On August 16, 2003, I was lying on my concrete bed in solitary, knowing sleep wouldn't come. Suddenly, the speaker in my cell turned on, and I heard the familiar sounds of a baseball game being broadcast. It was Major League Baseball's Saturday Game of the Week, live from Wrigley Field. The Los Angeles Dodgers were playing the Chicago Cubs.

One might think that I wouldn't care about baseball at that moment. After all, I was afraid and worried, accused of a crime I didn't commit, and sitting in solitary confinement with no access to my family. But right then, being able to listen to that baseball game meant everything to me. The only thing I could think when it came on was—yes!

I sat back for three hours and listened as two of the best pitchers in the game—Hideo Nomo for the Dodgers and Carlos Zambrano for the Cubs—battled it out. Was it a strange coincidence that Nomo was pitching this game, and he'd also pitched during that fateful game on May 12, 2003? As I listened to every pitch, I tried to forget about what was happening to me, but my emotions were all over the fucking place.

The Dodger's beat the Cubs, 10-5.

I spent the weekend in solitary confinement and was then put back in general population. Without a doubt, the Dodger's game got me through those days.

And then, I was transferred to Pitchess Detention Center, 'Wayside," AGAIN.

Wayside consists of several sections: Eastmax, Northmax, and Supermax. I started out in Supermax and then was transferred to Eastmax, where my first worry was keeping what I was arrested for a secret.

"Man," I continuously thought, "if anyone finds out what I'm here for, it's over."

During this time. I did my best to make sure I was eating, however, apparently, I wasn't eating enough. I befriended a solid homie in Wayside named Joker, who I kept running into. Every time he saw me, he'd shake his head. "You're wasting away, man," he'd say. "Wasting away."

One day, we were let out into the yard, where there was a scale. So I checked my weight. At the time of my arrest, I weighed 185 pounds, but the scale now read 167. The stress and worry were eating me up, literally.

Insofar as being social, I tried to keep to myself, but even that can be dangerous in the prison system because you want to have at least one person watching your back. For me, that person was an inmate nicknamed Shotgun, who became my cellmate and friend.

Shotgun was as solid as they came. He was only there for a probation violation, 45 days, so he was a short timer. The more I got to know him, the more comfortable I felt in telling him my story, and I found that being able to tell someone was a relief. Holding it all inside had been a huge burden on my shoulders.

Shotgun was dedicated to exercise, and we began working out together. This distracted me from my negative thoughts, and it helped me sleep. Paying attention to my mental and physical health, I ate most of my food and tried to exercise as much as I could when we were let out into the yard to walk, jog, or play basketball.

When not working out, we played cards, which gave me another opportunity to put on a little weight. Shotgun and I would make a good ole county spread—ramen noodles, crushed chips, leftover hard-boiled breakfast eggs, bread, mayo, mustard, and hot sauce. This was as good as it got in there.

The food sucked in Wayside, and I'm sure that's the case in prisons everywhere. Another thing true of the prison system is that there is nowhere you can go without being face to face with racial tensions. Three-quarters of the population consisted of blacks and Hispanics, followed by the smaller groups that included whites and "Piasas," which were Mexicans who were not born in the U.S.

For example, when you used the bathroom, which sometimes happened to be on the black's side, there were rules.

I was extremely vigilant because I knew that if I got into a fight, the LAPD and district attorney would use that against me to prove that I was a violent person. Actually, I almost felt like they were counting on it. Because race riots were common, I had to stay on my toes to keep that from happening, which led to many sleepless nights.

And one particular situation spiked that tension.

There were four phones in the dorm—two belonging to the blacks, and two were shared by the Hispanics and whites. Now, it's not hard to grasp that many of the calls that inmates made ended in anger— they got bad news from court, found out that their girlfriends were cheating on them, or were upset with their family for not sending them money. When that happened, they expressed their anger by slamming the phones against the receivers.

Well, phones aren't indestructible, and they could only take so much before the damage took its toll. Eventually, only one of the four phones was working, which meant that there was just one phone for more than a hundred inmates. This did not help matters at all. About a month in, the racial tensions had reached their limits, and we all knew that a riot was about to pop off. There was no way around it. And if—no, when—a riot began, there was no telling what would happen. Actually, in such a scenario, anything could happen.

I was somehow able to get to the one working phone to call my family.

"I just want you to know that I love you," I told Alma.

"What's wrong?" she asked. "You sound strange."

"Something bad is going to happen, and I just wanted you to know that I love you all very much."

But something bad didn't happen that night. Something good did.

Right before getting ready for lights out, which is when everything would have gone down, deputies stormed in.

"Everyone on their fucking bunks, facedown!", they screamed, herding us toward our beds. "Now!"

We did as we were told, and then we were ordered to strip down to our boxers. From there, we were marched into the hallway, where we discovered the air conditioning had been turned up. For the next hour, we were left shivering in the stone hallway, as deputies searched the dorm.

"Alright," came the next order after we were walked back to the dorm. "Lay face down on your bunks."

"Alright, motherfuckers. you guys want to kill each other, go right ahead! We found 57 shanks in the dorm!" the deputy screamed.

I knew that our side had 30, so that meant that the black inmates had 27. So, yeah, shit would've been bad.

I also knew that God was looking out for all of us that night—as He always is.

But the only thing the dorm raid did was unarm us. With the issue of the broken phones still unresolved, tensions were sure to escalate once again, and likely quickly.

"The pen is mightier than the sword," or, in this case, the knife. I'm not sure what made me think of it, but when that phrase popped into my head, it didn't leave. And although I wasn't quite sure what it meant in this situation, it kept repeating itself as if it were trying to tell me something.

So, I grabbed an almighty sword—or, in this case, a pen and wrote a letter to the Sargeant.
In the letter, I explained that the phones were damaged and shared how much the five or ten minutes talking to our families meant to us. If they wanted to relieve the tension in our dorm, they needed to do something about the phones.

I went on to say that some of us were looking at 5, 10, 15, or even 20-plus years, and we desperately needed the phones to curb the accompanying stress. I urged him to put in a work order to fix the phones or to replace them, saying it would go a long way to ease tensions.

In order for this letter to carry any weight, I knew it needed signatures—and the more, the better. So, I did something a little risky and asked the other inmates to sign it. Not sure how that request would go over, I was hesitant at first, but, surprisingly, about three-quarters of the inmates grabbed the letter and added their name to the bottom.

"Give me that shit," they'd say, quickly adding their name to the list, "I'll sign that motherfucker." Soon, we had more than eighty signatures. But when it came time to send the letter to the Sargeant, I was warned not to.

"Why?" I asked.

"Because they will fuck with you if you do," I was told. "You'll be a troublemaker, trying to disrupt their program."

While his words had merit, I wasn't ready to back down. I'd come this far and wanted to see it through. The next morning, an inmate who was going to court slid the envelope under the Sergeant's door. It was done.

A few days later, a deputy came to the door and yelled out, "Catalan!"

"Yeah?" I stood up from my bunk.

"Roll up your shit," he ordered.

The inmate who had warned me stood by, shaking his head.

"I told you," he said. "I told you."

He was right. The deputies were fucking with me using intimidation tactics. I figured whatever was going to happen had to happen. After all, I was looking at a fucking murder charge; what else could they do to me?

After they tried to intimidate me, I was escorted to a four-man cell, which would serve as my new temporary home. Going from a larger, overpopulated dorm to a 10' x 10' box takes a little getting used to, but at least there wasn't as much commotion, so I got a little relief. There was nothing I could do about it, so I settled in.

About a week later, I was making my way to the bus for my court date and passed by my old dorm. One of the inmates saw me and ran to the dorm window.

"Juan!" I heard someone yell,

"What's up?" I gestured with my head.

"Look," he pointed. When I peeked inside, I saw four brand new phones.

"You did it." he beamed.
Wow, I thought, amazed that something had actually been done. The pen, indeed, was mightier than the sword.

When in jail, the main priority is to keep busy, and with that, you have a few choices. First, there is court, which will take a lot of time. In fact, most of the day will be spent getting ready, being transported, and waiting, all for a ten-minute court appearance. Then you reverse the process. You leave in the morning, spend ten minutes in court, and come back late afternoon.

When I would finally get to the hallway just outside of the courtroom, Todd would pop out and brief me on what was going to happen. It was just a bit of back-and-forth interaction and then, boom, all done. Todd would say, "See you next time," and that was it.

Because the days are long and the justice system is slow, you learn patience. As day after day passed, I would reflect back on my life. I'm a big believer in karma, so for the life of me, I couldn't understand why I was there. What did I do to deserve this? Is my life really going to end here? Am I going to get sent to Death Row and be given the lethal injection?

If you let these thoughts fester, they grow into scary scenarios that will consume you. So, day in and day out, it was a constant struggle to try to keep calm and not let my mind run wild. It's difficult because when you're behind bars, it's easy to think that time stops. But it only stops for you. The outside world is still running full tilt.

The other options inmates have to keep busy include school and church. I did both.

Growing up Catholic, our parents took us to church on Sundays. But going to a Hispanic Catholic Church was like going to an event. You could never hear the priest's message because there were so many small children crying all the time. To me, going to church meant sitting there with my parents and trying not to go to sleep. But church service in jail is different. It's similar to regular church, but you're not looking forward to it ending because you don't get to go home. When the service was over, it was back to your cell.

Occasionally, the church group had people come from the outside to talk to us, to help us get our lives turned around.

There were two older men who would come and tell their stories. When they were young, they were involved in gangs and were in and out of jail. They spoke about how giving their lives to Christ changed them for the better, and it showed. I believed them. Someone who takes time out of their day to try to save someone else's soul is truly doing God's work.

In jail, I always prayed to God to help me. I constantly asked for forgiveness for my sins. My mom gave me some scriptures to read, as well, including Psalms 23 and 91, which are about God's protection, which put my mind on ease.

My mom was good at keeping me grounded while I was locked up. I would share with her my frustrations and fears, and as calm as could be, she would respond with the Word of God. Like I said earlier, my mom had often been ridiculed for her lack of education or lack of etiquette, but when it came to speaking about God from the heart, she had a gift. She reminded me that God would not allow this injustice to prosper and that the truth would set me free.

As I mentioned, I also went to school while in jail. I never graduated from high school, which bothered me, but while attending school in jail, something lit inside me. It then clicked that I had allowed my education to take a backseat, and I felt regret for it. How could I have been so irresponsible to not care about getting an education? I couldn't have been more wrong about education not being important. It was then that I made a promise to myself and to God that if I ever got out of this problem, I would go back and get my high school diploma.

It's ironic how the system works. Jail is supposed to help and rehabilitate people who make mistakes, but the sad truth is that it is a place where dreams and hopes fade into the abyss. I was able to compare adult jail with juvenile jail, and I can say that as an adult the system is meant to keep you down. I think it's designed that way.

Between school, court, and church, you spend your time trying to survive. I saw many fights, was involved in one riot, and had too many close calls to count. Violence of any kind, especially prison violence, plays with the psyche. There is nowhere to run or hide. There is no one coming to help you. Once you hear a grown man scream for help, you will never unhear it.

Visitations are so important in keeping morales up, but getting my family to visit was challenging. Although I missed my daughters, I couldn't stand the idea of my two little girls being anywhere near this place. Still, Alma did bring them occasionally.

One time, Alma was visiting with the girls, and since we couldn't physically touch each other, we had to talk between what seemed like a wall of glass. Melissa was six years old at the time and would point to where I was.

"I want to go over there with Daddy," she'd say. "I want to go over there."

That killed me. It broke my heart.

Talking to Todd on the phone wasn't any easier. When he asked how I was holding up, my only answer was, "Get me out of here."
Todd and I went over and over the night of the murder. I told him I believed I was at the Dodgers game the night of the murder, and not only was I there, but I also thought we had been filmed and that I might have even walked in front of the camera.

"Do you still have the tickets to the game?" Todd asked.

"Of course," I answered.

Hearing that, his reaction was one of pure excitement. He instructed Alma to look for them but not to touch them. His level of confidence about the entire situation was contagious, and I found myself feeling more confident, too.

"I'm going to get you out of here," he said. "And when I do, there will be people all over the country that will want to talk to you."

"I don't care about that," I pleaded. "Just please get me out of here."

I almost lost it when I talked to Alma and she said she couldn't find the Dodger's tickets.

"What do you mean, you can't find them?" I panicked. "They've got to be there. My life depends on it."

When Alma found the tickets later in a dresser drawer, she called Todd immediately.

As Todd was preparing my defense, Beth Silverman, the District Attorney, was preparing the prosecution.

"I don't want this to concern you, Juan," Todd said, "but Silverman has never lost a murder case."

For about 90 days, I was transferred from Wayside to L.A County and back again to Wayside, which, once again, held double the number of inmates it was designed for.

When the majority of inmates are looking at sentences of 10 or 20 years or life, anger and hate are everywhere. Being locked up with inmates who had no shot of getting out or didn't give a fuck was beyond dangerous.

Todd worked hard on my case, and he had an update for me every couple of weeks. And I was always anxious to call him to get that update.

Todd was digging into my alibi and any proof that could be found that connected me to that game. He had contacted the L.A. Dodgers, who were beyond gracious and helped him with anything he needed. He even met with Sam Fernandez, General Counsel and a Senior Vice President for the Dodgers, and Sam was a godsend. He first showed Todd some basic footage from Dodger Stadium that night, but it was too blurry. Sam then provided him with information about HBO, who was the group filming that day. So, Todd actually had to go to the offices where CURB YOUR ENTHUSIASM is produced to look over the footage from the game. Now, I must mention all this did not come without resistance, but they did set it up so Todd would go into their offices to review it himself. Todd told me to call him in a week to see if he found anything.

That might have been the longest week of my life. I called my family, and they prayed that Todd would find me on that video. Some of the inmates who knew what was going on even wished me luck.

When the day finally came, my heart was pounding when I picked up the phone.

Time slowed down. It seemed like an eternity for the receptionist to get Todd on the phone. When he got on the line, I said ONE expectant word—Hello.

"Dude," he said.

"Yeah?"

"You're on tape," Todd replied.

I could count on one hand the number of times I'd ever felt what I felt at that moment—pure joy.

I hung up and I turned to the other inmates.

"I'm on tape," I announced.

"Fuck yeah, homie!" was all I heard.

The only thing running through my mind was that this was over. It was finally over. I could even envision myself walking out of jail the next day and hugging my family. But Todd quickly brought me back to earth.

Alright Mazzone had his chat, and Ray King ready to go to work. Brian Jordan grounded to short, flied to center. Up there with the bases loaded. He has a half-dozen grand slams and the last one last year against the Giants. Jordan tonight 0 for 2. AND THAT'S A WILD PITCH. It comes back toward Lopez, but everybody moves up 90 feet. And the Brave lead is 4-3. Now the Dodgers have the tying run at third and a possible go ahead run at second, and I mean that was wild. That run is charged to Reynolds. For the veteran Ray King, that would be his second wild pitch. So now first base is open, and I think they're going to take the bat out of Jordan's hands and walk him intentionally. It will be the third walk given to the Dodgers in the inning. And Mike Kincade, who walked and homered against Shane Reynolds, is coming up. So in a moment, the Dodgers for the second time in the inning will have the bases loaded. Up north, Montreal has the bases loaded with two out and Jose Vidro at the plate, and the Dodgers know how good a hitter Vidro is. Meanwhile, Bobby Cox is gonna go back to the mound. So Ray King comes in wild, walks McGriff, wild pitches a run over. They walked Jordan intentionally, and Trey Hodges, the right hander, had been throwing. So let's watch Bobby as he gets to the mound. King shaking his head, and that'll do it. And we'll be right back.

Vin Scully, Dodger's Stadium, May 12, 2003

CHAPTER SEVEN

The Phone Call

*N*omo has walked seven. Chipper Jones hit back to the box, grounded out, and then lined out deep to right in the fifth inning. Ball one, nice save by LoDuca. So Chipper, just the opposite of Gary Sheffield. Where Sheffield has had tremendous success against Nomo, Chipper has struggled up to the moment. One ball, no strikes. Ball two. When Chipper was very young, his dad fashioned a piece of lightweight PVC pipe to use as a bat. And he's grown up and swinging that Louisville Slugger. Ball three, so Nomo now starting I'm sure to be fighting it. He's been fighting his control all night. Andy Ashby is up in the Dodger bullpen again. Three and 0 to Chipper Jones. That's in there. Chipper's from a little town in Florida, Pierson, Florida, and believe it or not, Pierson Florida is the fern capital of the world. So as a kid, he worked in a fern packing shed. High fly ball but very playable, very high but not deep, so Jordan has to come in to get it. So for Nomo, it's amazing he can't get Sheffield out, but he sure can take care of Chipper Jones. Chipper Jones going back to the dugout is 0 for 3 tonight. So for Chipper against Nomo, he has 2 hits in 34 at-bats. And he's just fed up looking at Hideo.

Vin Scully, Dodger's Stadium, May 12, 2003

"Right now," Todd said, "the deal from Silverman, the District Attorney, is if you plead guilty, you get life in prison without the possibility of parole."

"Think about that for a second, Juan. The best option, the outcome they will give you for playing ball, is life behind bars."

"But you've got the video, I mean, that—."

"We need more."

Todd wanted to go through their evidence to pick it apart and see what he could and couldn't use for our defense. Aside from the sole eyewitness, Martha had been in contact with multiple friends earlier that day. Todd wanted to interview everyone and leave no stone unturned.

So that's what he did.

***

Inmates will do anything to avoid thinking of the free world, because it will only drive them crazy. They will lift weights, fight, gamble, pace, read. Anything. Because if they don't, they'll begin to wonder if their girlfriend is cheating on them or if their kids are getting used to them not being around.

However, I didn't bother to try to avoid it. I thought about my two daughters all day long. I thought about taking them to school, about helping them with their homework, and about the possibility that they would grow up without me. Then I would think of my own family; my brother was locked up, too, so that meant there was no one to help my dad at our family's shop. Naturally, all of this made me sad. It made me fucking angry. It's one thing to break the law, knowing you are guilty and are now paying the price. But it's entirely different when you are innocent and taken away from your family while your existence on the outside is being erased— HELL NO.

One might think any opportunity to get out of jail would be welcomed, but I hated going to court. One time when I was right outside the courtroom, several female inmates were walking through.

"Don't look over there," the deputy instructed them. "He's a murderer." Picking up their pace, they quickly passed by.

Another time, a deputy took me to an isolated tank.

"Hey," he said holding the door.

"Yeah?"

"They got you."

"What are you talking about?" I asked

"They found your DNA at the crime scene," he grinned.

"That's impossible," I said.

But he just smiled as he shut the door.

Another time, there was an earthquake while I was in the cell waiting for court. We were on the ninth floor of a city building, and I was locked inside a small room that was shaking from the quake. Looking through the crack, I was able to see a deputy, and judging by his face, he was shook.

"Hey," I yelled, noticing the shaking was getting worse. "Get me out of here."

Frightened, he looked at me and then ran out of the room.

Court hearings were always the same for me. I was not allowed to say a word, just sit there, just be there—but it was a different type of being there.

Todd had interviewed several of Martha's acquaintances. One was the eyewitness that had claimed I was the shooter. His name was Juan Ibanez, and he didn't speak English. There were also neighbors who claimed they saw me shoot her.

With the stress building up, I lost it during a three-way call between me, Todd, and Alma.

"MY PARENTS PAID YOU ALL THAT MONEY," I screamed to Todd. "IT MIGHT NOT BE A LOT OF MONEY TO YOU, BUT IT IS TO US!"

"Juan," he said, "I understand you're frustrated and stressed, but—."

"I'M ON THE VIDEO," I screamed. "You have the Dodger's ticket. What else do you need?"

"Did you buy anything at the game?" Todd asked.

"What?"

"A hot dog, a beer, anything?"

I told him I had, but I knew Todd was looking for credit card purchases that he could track, and I had used cash.

"What about a phone call?" Alma asked.

"A phone call? What phone call?"

"I called Juan at the end of the night," Alma explained. "While he was at the stadium."

I could almost see Todd's ears perk up with that news. Excited, he went back to work.

The crazy thing was that, at that time, cell phone providers destroyed all calls and text data after three months. Verizon, AT&T, T-Mobile—they all did—all except Nextel. Nextel was the only provider that kept this information for six months.

To my saving grace, I had Nextel. And it had been about five and a half months since the game. Had I been with any other provider or if it had been just a couple weeks longer, the information we needed would have been gone. CHILLS.

The information was there, and we knew it, but we needed to get it from Nextel in order to use it in court. To do that, Todd had to get a court order signed by a judge, and he had to do it quickly before the information was destroyed. Again, Todd put on his cape and got the signed order, and to our excitement and relief, Nextel provided him with my cell phone information. This is just one example of how everything was almost like a miracle and had to line up like dominoes in order to prove my innocence.

The Nextel cell tower that picked up my call was located at (ironically) the Los Angeles Police Academy, which is across the street from the stadium. Todd also discovered that this cell tower had a one-mile radius, so had I not been in the area of Dodger Stadium, the cell tower would've never picked up the call.

Interestingly enough, Todd learned about this cell phone tower hack from working on the infamous O.J Simpson double murder case when he was right out of law school.

So, we now had the game tickets, the HBO Curb Your Enthusiasm video, which was time coded at 9:11 pm, and the final piece of the puzzle, which was the cell phone recorded at 10:11—sufficient proof that I was still at Dodger Stadium and not circling around Martha's neighborhood, as alleged and corroborated by witnesses and Martha's neighbors.

Todd now felt confident enough to go up against Silverman and the LAPD with the evidence we had.

Todd's goal was to get this case thrown out at the preliminary hearing, which is unheard of in murder cases. But the biggest reason for wanting it to be thrown out before a trial was due to the legal fees. If this case went to trial, he would need to charge my family $75,000, which we wouldn't have been able to afford. Besides, going to trial was risky. I know I certainly didn't want to think about what could happen if it came to that.

The craziest part, which is now public knowledge, is that Silverman only had ONE piece of information that was true. I was, indeed, in the area of the murder around the time of the murder. How? What are the chances that I would be in the block where a murder took place, and after being accused of committing that murder, it just so happens that I was within walking distance of the crime? I have had many sleepless nights over this exact thought.

Throughout this time, I had never seen the "sole eyewitness" who pointed me out to the LAPD. Outside of the courtroom, in the judge's chambers, Beth Silverman immediately voiced her concerns over the high-profile case. She mentioned that since this case was about the murder of a witness, she was now concerned about their star witness. The truth was neither Silverman nor the LAPD gave a fuck about Ibanez's safety. Since Todd had a crew filming the proceedings, Silverman asked the court to not allow them to show or mention their star witness. In his ruling, Judge Dunn ordered that their star witness be referred to only by his middle name, "Manuel."

Todd, being the amazing attorney he is, countered with his concerns about "Manuel" seeing me in court for the first time, apart from the one time he'd allegedly seen me on night of the murder. Todd wanted me out of their witness's view just long enough for Todd to cross examine him regarding my characteristics by "voir dire," which is where the attorney asks about their background before their testimony is heard. He tried several methods, from having me removed entirely from the courtroom to placing me behind a blackboard that was already in the courtroom, in order to shield me from Manuel. Judge Dunn rejected those requests, but they finally agreed with Todd covering me up with his suit coat.

When proceedings got underway on the first day, Silverman again started complaining that Todd hadn't handed over any discovery he had regarding my defense. Judge Dunn asked Todd if he had any witnesses and said that the people were entitled to that information through reciprocal discovery. Todd fired back, stating that as he understood penal code under 1054, he had no right to share any discovery until 30 days before trial and especially not before the preliminary hearing. Silverman and Pinner played their cat and mouse game by sharing their limited information with Todd literally the weekend before the preliminary hearing, yet here was Silverman threatening a motion to continue because Todd hadn't shared his discovery.

But Silverman got what she wanted when Judge Dunn asked me to waive my right to a continuous preliminary hearing. She then instructed the people to call their first witness. Todd interrupted by asking for me to be unhandcuffed, since I was going to have his jacket over my head. Judge Dunn agreed to have ONE hand uncuffed. Todd then asked the court to address one more thing—Martha's mother, who was crying uncontrollably in the audience. I never ONCE blamed that lady for her emotions because it was not her fault that the LAPD falsely accused and arrested me, putting me on trial for her daughter's murder.

When I walked into the preliminary hearing on the first day, I was as nervous as could be. Then Todd made it worse when he walked up to me, obviously worried.

 "What?" I asked.

"Juan," he said, "when we go into court, do not look to the left of the courtroom, just look straight ahead."

"Why?" I asked.

"Because Martha's family is in the courtroom, and they are wailing."

I wasn't sure what to feel. I knew I was innocent, but this family was being told by the LAPD and the District Attorney that I was their daughter's killer.

I walked into the courtroom, my hands in cuffs. As I headed to the defendant's chair, my peripheral vision picked up Martha's family, sobbing uncontrollably.

I was taken to my seat, uncuffed, and sat, looking straight ahead.

After Todd spoke briefly with the judge and the then district attorney, the hearing began.

First up, Detective Martin Pinner took the stand.

DA Silverman began by asking Pinner what his assignment within the LAPD was. Pinner replied he was assigned to the North Hollywood

Detective Homicide Unit. Silverman asked if he was the investigating officer of the Puebla case and the homicide case outside of her home. Yes, he was. Silverman then asked if Pinner was present during a May, 2003 preliminary hearing when Martha took the stand.

Pinner not only acknowledged this, but he agreed that he had seen me in the courtroom on the day in question. Silverman was setting up the allegation that I was there to intimidate the witness.

Now, as I said earlier, we were there because my brother, Mario, called nonstop asking for us, his family, to show up to the preliminary hearing to support him. Mario explained how the judge viewed the family's presence and support as a positive. Since my dad did nothing but work, my mom did not do heights, and my sisters were all younger, that only left me.

Then Silverman brought up another homicide that had nothing to do with my brother or me. Silverman's specialty was high-profile gang murder cases, and my brother was a co-defendant in another murder case, but that is only because his incompetent attorney could not get a motion to sever the cases, which would have led to separate jury trials.

Silverman then brought up a phone book that the police found in Martha's bedroom and highlighted two pages of it to coincide with their theory of me being the shooter. What they never mentioned was that the phone book included multiple gangs and gang members' names and phone numbers. In reality, the possibilities as to who shot Martha were endless.

Silverman and Pinner tried several things. First, to shrink my height second, to add facial features that were not there; and third, to make a car that didn't match the description, but that I drove for a short while, become the murder getaway car. Their efforts were actually disappointing and pathetic.

It was now Todd's turn to cross-examine Pinner, but instead, he had two of our witnesses to take the stand. He was about to put on what is called an affirmative defense.

Todd first called the individual who was on the phone with Martha when the shooter was driving around her neighborhood. He testified about a small altercation between Martha and one of the guys who were with Manuel. Martha was mad because they brought a girl to her house that she didn't want there.

Then Todd went to work on Detective Pinner.

Todd began by asking Pinner about cell phone numbers and calls to verify the validity of times—in particular, the time the call was made from this individual to Puebla at 10:04 p.m. Todd was trying to establish that the information he was able to produce from the cell phone providers was solid and correct.

"Umm," Pinner said, "I did not personally correlate the information with the LAPD."

Todd asked Detective Martin Pinner to connect the dots regarding Martha's girlfriend being upset at Martha, and all the people who were present at Martha's house, as well as the testimony of Manuel stating he saw the would-be shooter driving around Martha's house at approximately 10:04 p.m. This was already known information, but Pinner could not provide it.

"Did you personally review the interview tapes, the witness statements, and information provided to you?"

"No."

"But Amador was a huge piece to this investigation, and you are the lead detective."

Todd asked about another tape of Ortega and if he had listened to it, to which he responded, "No."

"Did you listen to the tape of Alma Oseguera?"

"No."

"How about the tape of Trujillo?"

"No."

"How about the second tape of Amador?"

"No"

Todd grilled Detective Pinner, asking if he wrote any supplemental reports or notes or translations, what you would call normal detective work, all to which Pinner replied,

"No."

With that response, Todd shook his head. "Hmm, really?" he said to the detective.

Todd was relentless. He kept on pressing the lead homicide detective with tough questions that made Pinner uncomfortable. Naturally, Silverman objected often during these questions, so much so that Todd had to address the judge.

Todd even asked the judge if the detective could stop looking at the D.A. for help.

But the judge's response was disappointing and dismissive.

From where I was sitting, the prosecution did little preparation, possibly believing this was an open and shut case and they didn't need to. Instead, Silverman just objected to everything Todd said.

Then everything hit the boiling point.

Todd was so upset because he felt the hearing seemed to be one sided and unfair.

When Todd asked Detective Pinner if he had retrieved Manuel's cell phone records prior to Todd being forced to hand them over, Pinner replied with his favorite answer, "No." So he learned this information only when Todd provided it to the People. WOW, again. After so many objections by Silverman and agreements from the Judge, Todd addressed the court.

"Your Honor, I believe that it would go to his course of investigation and how he determined timelines, and things of that nature, about when the crime happened."

"Well, how he went about establishing the timeline. What relevance would that be?" the judge replied.

If you think Todd was pissed off at how the investigation had taken place, imagine how I felt.

When Judge Dunn ordered the people to call their first witness, Silverman called Manuel. Since he did not speak English, the translator interpreted the code of civil procedure. Silverman began by asking introductory questions.

"Did you know someone by the name of Martha Puebla?" Yes. "How did you know her?" and "How long had you known her?"

Silverman then focused on May 12, 2003, the night of the murder.

The witness, Manuel, stated that he was there around 10:30 p.m., alongside three other individuals, a female and two males. Manuel knew the two boys, but not the girl. Manuel described the situation, testifying that the two girls were arguing and the guys left Martha's house, leaving Manuel alone with Martha. As Manuel stood there for about half an hour talking to Martha, a dark black four-door car began circling the block. Manuel stated that the individual in this car walked past them to the corner and then turned and walked back toward them, twice.

When Martha was sitting on the curb and the individual was close by, Manuel stated this person walked up behind Martha and spoke.

"Who are you?" the individual asked. "Do I know you?"

Martha then replied, "It's me, Martha. You remember me."

Silverman asked Manuel what happened next.

"You don't know me," the shooter replied.

"He took out a handgun," Manuel said, "and shot her."

According to Manuel, the shooter was standing over Martha approximately three to four feet away and shot at her in a downward motion.

"So what did you do then?" Silverman asked Manuel.

"I started running," he answered. Manuel stated that the shooter chased him, but due to the shock of watching Martha get shot, he was not sure if the person was also shooting at him. When Manuel turned around, he saw the shooter heading back in the direction he came from.

Silverman then asked Manual to describe the shooter. Manuel stated that the shooter was Hispanic, a bit taller than he was. Silverman asked how tall Manuel was, and he said five foot five. He went on to say that the shooter was not fat and had a normal build. Manuel guessed his age to be between 20-26 years old. He also stated that the shooter was almost bald but had a big moustache that was fully grown. Manuel believed the shooter's weight was around 150 pounds, since Manuel weighed 140 pounds.

Claiming he didn't know what to do, Manuel said he called his friend, Sergio, to pick him up and take him to Ricardo's house, who was a friend who knew Martha well. When Manuel arrived, he explained what had happened. He never called the police out of fear, and being undocumented, he thought he would be in huge trouble. Ibanez didn't realize he dropped his phone at the scene, but the phone actually belonged to his boss.

The LAPD then had Manuel aid them with a police sketch and help the artist to come up with a composite drawing of the shooter.

Silverman then asked Manuel if the LAPD had shown him some photographs of suspects, to which he responded yes. From all the sets of photographs, Manuel stated he chose one that resembled the shooter. Silverman hammered the point of choosing a person from the photographs and him writing a note that read, "I saw when this person shoots Martha the night that she was killed." Silverman asked if Manuel was certain that the person he circled was, indeed, the shooter, to which Manuel responded. "Yes."

Judge Dunn then asked Todd if he wished to cross-examine the witness.

Todd began by asking Manuel his own round of introductory questions, then picked up where the shooter walked up to Martha. Todd asked Manuel how long he believed the shooter was standing there before he shot Martha and repeated the description of the car the shooter was in. Todd mentioned to Manuel that he had told police that he saw that car drive around three or four times. Todd then asked about his height, and to drive the point, he stood next to Manuel to compare heights. Since Todd is six feet tall, He was trying to show that if the shooter was, indeed, a little bit taller than six feet, he would have seemed much taller. Manuel had stated to the police that he believed the shooter was 5'5" to 5'7", but in court he said he now did not remember.

Todd then asked Manuel if he remembered telling his friend, Ricardo, that the shooter was bald, chubby, and 5'7". Manuel answered no, he didn't recall that. Todd then aggressively attacked Manuel's description of the shooter's height.

"Objection, your honor."

And more times than not, Judge Dunn seemed to favor the prosecution. Todd then asked Manuel to repeat the description of the shooter he had given to the police.

"That he was a Hispanic guy, that was a little bit taller than me, a little bit fuller than me, and that his hair was short and he had a moustache," Manuel stated.

Todd asked the witness if the shooter looked like a gang member, and Manuel replied yes.

Todd had nothing further to add, so Judge Dunn asked that the jacket that was covering me be removed. Silverman then continued with her examination of their witness. Silverman only asked Manuel if the person he saw shoot Martha was in the courtroom.

"Yes," Manuel replied. He looked over to me and pointed me out.

What the fuck are you doing? I thought.

Silverman had nothing further.

Todd continued with his cross examination. He asked about Manuel's cell phone and where he got it from. He asked Manuel if he contacted Martha with that phone, to which Manuel responded yes. Todd started putting together a timeline for the day in question. He established that Manuel and other friends had planned to drive to Martha's later that evening. Manuel brought a female along, as well, only to have Martha act aggressively to her. Martha even cursed Manuel's friends for bringing the girl with them.

While this was going on, Manuel stated he saw the shooter's car driving by. Todd then confirmed that all the people that drove to Martha's house left, leaving only Manuel with Martha.

Todd asked a couple more questions, and then Judge Dunn ordered a break for lunch.

When we returned, Todd went back to the timeline. Todd asked Manuel if, when he saw the would-be shooter, he believed that he had any business with Martha. Manuel replied, "No," and stated that he thought he was a guy walking by and never imagined anything like that would happen.

Todd then tried to ask Manuel questions about information he gave to the LAPD about Martha. He pointed out that since Manuel ran after the shooting, the only way the LAPD found him was because he dropped his cell phone, and the police were able to use it to track him down. One of the most shocking things for me to hear was Todd asking Manuel about the LAPD showing him some six packs of mug shots, only to find out that he had ORIGINALLY selected two other guys!

Manuel circled the mug shot, signed it, and wrote a statement about him seeing these people shoot Martha. Not only that, but the LAPD actually accused Manuel of either killing Martha himself or setting it up, or worse yet, being coached to accept my picture on a six pack! Another interesting fact was that Manuel was in jail earlier in the year for methamphetamine. YUP. METHAMPHETAMINE.

Their star witness was not only a meth user but had been coached by the LAPD to choose me from that six pack of photos. Todd exposed that.

The next witnesses were the custodians of records for both Verizon and Nextel.

First to testify was Michael Downs from Nextel Communications, which was my cell phone provider. This witness testified to the multiple cell numbers that were used by all parties involved on the night of May 12th. He stated who they belonged to and how long particular calls were. The most important call of all was an incoming call to my cell phone from Alma at 10:11 p.m. I remember that call clearly as we were walking out of the stadium.

Todd asked the Nextel representative what cell tower this call was received from. Michael responded that it was the cell tower NCA6581R, which belonged to the L.A.P.D, (how ironic). The cell tower was also located across the street from Dodger Stadium at the police academy. There were a few more calls made from my cell phone, which Todd purposely put on the record to establish my timeline.

Once Todd finished, Silverman crossed examined. She asked how far cell towers could pick up calls. The Nextel rep responded that all cell towers are different. He said some towers need to be next door and others as far as 10 miles. She asked about the police academy cell tower and its range.

"Probably like a mile or less," the Nextel rep responded. Silverman also asked if there were any calls made or received between 10:11 and 10:45, which was the supposed murder window. There were none.

Another key witness to take the stand was Tim Gibbons, who was a producer for HBO's Curb Your Enthusiasm. Todd went right in and asked his occupation and whether the show was filming on May 12, 2003. Tim provided his title and stated that yes, indeed, they were filming that night at Dodger Stadium. Todd went into detail about requesting footage from them and about the difficult efforts and legalities one had to go through to get Tim, Curb Your Enthusiasm, and most important, Larry David to provide Todd the footage.

As the footage was played in court, both Todd and Tim went back and forth about what and who was on the footage. Tim pointed out Larry David, who is the star of Curb Your Enthusiasm and was shown walking up and down the aisle. Todd pointed out the time code across the raw footage pf the video, which is never shown in the final product but is used for production reasons. In another shot of the raw footage, Tim pointed out Larry talking to Bob Einstein, who was famously known as Super Dave Osbourne. This specific scene was shot over and over.

Todd asked why there were multiple shots of the same scene, and Tim responded because they were filming during a live baseball game and it would have been impossible to have the typical number of cameras during filming due to all the spectators. Todd pointed out all the details surrounding this scene, including the time the scene was shot.

After this, Judge Dunn adjourned court until the following day, which was Thursday, December 18, 2003. Handcuffed again, I was being escorted out of the room into the holding tank when Martha's mother yelled out, "Nunca te voy a perdonar por lo que le hiciste a mi hija!" (I'll never forgive you for what you did to my daughter!) Her words felt like a knife straight to my heart.

On the second day of the preliminary hearing, Todd was convinced he would prove my innocence and ultimately get me out for Christmas, something he promised my daughter, Melissa, he would do. But we also knew that Silverman and the LAPD would try every trick they could to prevent me from being released.

When court began, Silverman complained about Todd putting up an "alibi defense" and stated that he had not turned over evidence to them. After putting up our evidence to this point, the "People" claimed they had been completely blindsided. Silverman asked for a continuance on the grounds that Todd hadn't provided them with this information. Todd, having spoken to other attorneys, could not find any law supporting that requirement. Therefore, he argued that he had no such duty to disclose the evidence, considering the fact that we were only in the preliminary hearing.

Judge Dunn interrupted, asking Todd if, based on the defense he was establishing, he was going to ask her to dismiss the case, to which Todd replied, "Absolutely." The judge stated that since it was a special circumstance murder trial, she could not see how he expected the People, in good faith, to not to have a chance to review the discovery and prepare accordingly.

Todd responded that, as he understood the law, he did not have a duty under the code to disclose all discovery. He had his reasons and had discussed them with Silverman beforehand. He was adamant that I was factually innocent, to which Judge Dunn again chimed in, saying she would not entertain a motion to dismiss until the People had an opportunity to go over all the evidence.

"Fine. How much time do they need?" Todd asked.

Silverman complained that they did not have the videotape that we played in court and that she did not have any of the evidence that Todd provided. Silverman went as far as saying that precious court time was being wasted and that someone was sitting in custody on very serious charges.

EXCUSE ME? She was now worried about me? Sure, okay. Silverman then threatened to take up possible sanctions for those reasons.

Judge Dunn asked Todd what else he had that the People had not seen, and he read off a list of items. The Judge then asked Silverman how much time she needed to go over the discovery, to which she replied that she needed at least a week.

"That is incredibly excessive, your honor," Todd argued. Judge Dunn explained that since Christmas was in one week and the courts would be closed, so the preliminary hearing had to be rolled over into the new year, 2004.

Todd was furious.

"I don't want my client in jail for another day, your honor," he said. "Much less until next year."

The judge scolded Todd, stating that if he had turned over all discovery, there wouldn't have been a continuance. Todd wanted to continue the hearing the next day and even said he would explain the cell phone records to Silverman. Judge Dunn gave the court a recess to see if Silverman could be persuaded to continue the case the following day.

Coming out of the recess, the judge asked Silverman if they had come to an agreement, and, of course, she stated they had not. She also said she would be off the last week of December and Detective Pinner would need a couple of weeks to look over all the evidence. Looking at the calendar, the judge offered to continue the hearing until January 5th or 7th.

Beyond furious, Todd was now livid. He asked to be heard and mentioned some cases that he believed held precedence in this instance. The court jargon went back and forth between the parties like a game of ping pong. Todd was positive that he did not have to hand over our evidence, but Judge Dunn said otherwise. The more the argument went on, the more disheartened Todd became. The more disheartened he became, the more he fought the continuance. The judge remained firm, basically saying that it was due to his own doing that she had no choice but to grant the continuance.

When Silverman asked if we wanted the 5th or the 7th, Todd chose the soonest date possible—the 5th. Because of the continuance, I had to give up my right to have my preliminary hearing heard in one continuous, interrupted session. On the same note, I also had to give up my right to have an early preliminary hearing so we would be able to conclude the hearing on January 5th, as well. Lastly, Judge Dunn asked me if I waived my right to be sentenced in the other felony matter until January 5th, to which, of course, I agreed.

Feeling like he'd been shamed by Judge Dunn for not disclosing our evidence, Todd was ordered to turn over all evidence so the district attorney could review it and come up with a proper defense.

Having granted a two-week continuance, Judge Dunn's ruling meant

I would be locked up for Christmas and New Year.

I would not be home for Christmas.

The hearing wrapped up, and I went back into the hellhole of the LA County Jail. Alma later told me that once they were outside the courtroom, Todd got on his knees and, with tears in his eyes, he apologized to Melissa for not being able to get me out like he'd said he would.

But Todd was not going to let what happened on that day slide. He was more determined than ever to prove that he was not under any legal obligation to share our evidence at this stage of the proceedings.

Todd filed what is known as a writ, explaining what happened that day in court. Again, though, we were only a week from Christmas and New Years, and the courts were closed for the most part during the holidays. Todd still pressed forward to get the ten-page writ reviewed and ruled upon. By the time Todd heard back, it was literally a day or two from our court date of January 5th. But Todd got the ruling he wanted—and deserved. The court that reviewed the writ came back in his favor, proving that he was right—he did not, in fact, have to share our evidence during a preliminary hearing.

If nothing else, Todd had the satisfaction of knowing he was doing everything by the book, which sadly could not be said for the other side.

On my end, the two weeks leading up to the new court date were the slowest two weeks of my life. And do you want to know what the LAPD and Silverman did to investigate me during this two-week break? Ready?

Pinner asked another detective IF THERE WAS A DODGER GAME ON MAY 12TH!

Shaking my damn head.

I was beyond nervous when they brought me back to court on January 5th, but this time something was different. In previous hearings, there were a handful of people in the courtroom, but now it was jam packed. Word had gotten around.

As Judge Dunn opened the hearing, Todd asked if the court saw the ruling that came back from the writ he filed. Judge Dunn replied that she had not. Feeling absolved, Todd informed that the court held that the order of discovery was erroneous and that the People were ordered to vacate.

Silverman was asked if she had seen a copy of the ruling, to which she sheepishly replied, "Yes." Just to give you an idea of their shadiness, when Todd told the court that they still had copies of our discovery, Silverman said the writ only said to return the original copies, but not the copies they had already made of our evidence. Just wow.

The hearing resumed with Detective Pinner on the stand.

Since I just touched on some of the main points between Pinner and Todd, I want you to hear this. The following is a piece of this interaction verbatim from actual transcripts:
Todd: Good morning.

Pinner: Good morning.

Todd: Did you determine the phone number that Martha Puebla used on the night of the… of her death?

Pinner: Yes.

Todd: What was that phone number?

Pinner: Area code (XXX) XXX-XXXX.

Todd: And did you determine that there was the ability for that particular phone to trap phone numbers that had called it through caller I.D?

Pinner: It's not called a trap, but I understand your reference. We downloaded the… or one of the other detectives downloaded the called I.D box by writing down the numbers that had called the home and looking at the caller I.D box and just jotting those numbers down.

Todd: And was one of the numbers that was on that caller I.D the number from Efrain Ortega?

Pinner: It was later determined to be Efrain Ortega, XXX-XXXX.

The court: Can I have that number again?

Pinner: (XXX) XXX-XXXX.

The court: Thank you.

Todd: Through those phone records that you got, did you determine, approximately, what time Mr. Ortega had talked to Martha Puebla?

Pinner: Yes.

Todd: What time was that?

Pinner: Can I check?

Todd: Certainly.

Pinner: 10:04 p.m. or 2204.

Todd: And that time corresponds with the records that were produced, pursuant to subpoena by either Nextel or Verizon, in this case on the 18th of October.

Silverman: Well, I object. That would call for a conclusion.

The court: Sustained.

Todd: You were in court when the evidence was presented from either Verizon or Nextel; is that correct?

Pinner: Yes.

Todd: Did you see the reports produced with the phone number (XXX) XXX-XXXX.

Pinner: Yes.

Todd: And according to those phone numbers that you saw here in court, and I assume that you reviewed over the last two weeks?

Pinner: Yes.

Todd: Did it appear that the phone call that you took at 10:04 p.m. off the caller I.D was also identical to the records that you saw that were produced by myself, and through either Verizon or Nextel, in this matter?

Pinner: I understand your question. I didn't personally look at the caller I.D box. It was written down for me by somebody else. That was 2204. I do not recollect right off the top of my head just from the records, but I understand that it's… I have seen them, but I don't remember right off the top of my head if it was accurate as to the records provided through you, to us, on December 18th.

Todd: All right. May I ask the clerk to provide me with the exhibits in this matter?
The court: Sure.

Todd: Showing you exhibit "C" for the phone number (XXX) XXX-XXXX. Is this Efrain Ortega's phone number?

Pinner: Yes.

Todd: The call was at 22:04 and 24 seconds?

Pinner: Yes.

Todd: And lasted 346 seconds or approximately five-and-a-half minutes?

Pinner: Yes.

Todd: And the number called was Martha's number, (XXX) XXX-XXXX?

Pinner: Yes.

Todd: All right. So this corresponds to the notes that you saw in the recording, the investigation, about when Efrain called Martha?

Pinner: Yes.

Todd: Now, you were aware that Mr. Ortega had overheard a phone conversation, or overheard some activity going on through Martha's phone; is that right?

Pinner: Yes.

Todd: When he made the call.

Pinner: Yes.

Todd: And he overheard at least one man's voice during the conversation?

Pinner: Yes.

Todd: And he also heard statements to the effect that, "Why did you bring that bitch here," or words to that effect; is that correct?

Pinner: Yes.

Todd: And based on your investigation in this matter, after getting the statements of Cecelia Amador and Ricardo Trujillo and Manuel, did you determine that the three of them present, or at the location of Martha Puebla's home, at the time of that conversation?

Silverman: Well, I'm going to object. That would call for speculation and conclusion.

The court: Sustained.

Todd: Through your investigation, did you determine that the three witnesses were at Martha's house at the time of Efrain's phone call?

Silverman: Same objection.

The court: Sustained.

Todd: Did you determine the whereabouts of Manuel at approximately, between 10:02 and 10:45 p.m. on the night of May 12th?

Pinner: Yes.

Todd: Where did you determine his whereabouts to be?

Pinner: Based on his statement he was outside Martha's on Case Street.

Todd: And between 10:02 and approximately 10:15, give or take a few minutes either way, did you determine where Cecelia Amador was, based on everything that you learned about this case?

The court: Sustained. It is the same question. It's calling for a conclusion.

Todd: Did you determine, through your investigation, that Martha was upset with Cecelia being at her house?

Silverman: Same objection.

The court: Sustained.

Todd: Did Cecelia Amador tell you that Martha was upset about her being at Martha's house?

Pinner: I never interviewed Cecelia Amador.

Todd: Did you ever listen to the tapes in this matter?

Pinner: No.

Todd: You provided me with 11 tapes on Thursday, the 9th or 10th… let me get the date correct. The 11th of December. Do you recall that?

Pinner: The 12th.

Todd: Was it Friday?

Pinner: Yes, sir.

Todd: All right. On Friday, the 12th of December, you provided me with those tapes. Is it your testimony that you have not listened to any of those tapes?

Pinner: No, that's not my testimony.

Todd: All right. Which tapes did you listen to?

Pinner: I've listened to parts and portions of some of them, not all of them. Some of them I have not listened to at all.

Todd: All right.

Pinner: But specifically Cecelia Amador I haven't listened to period.

Todd: All right. You provided me with two tapes of Juan, is that correct?

Pinner: Yes.

Todd: And tape number 309790 which was a tape that was made on or about September 15, if my memory serves me, correctly.

Pinner: Well, it was in September.

Todd: And the other tape, which is 1 of 1 that you provided to me which is tape number 292948, that was made on May 13 or 14 of 2002?

Pinner: 2003.

Todd: Yes. Thank you. 2003. Did you listen to this tape?

Pinner: No. Parts of it, not the entire thing.

Todd: Which portions did you listen to?

Silverman: Well, I'm going to object. That would call for a cumulative answer.

The court: Well, I'm not sure that he can answer that question. You are going to need to rephrase it.

Todd: Well, there is some different portions and subject areas on this tape, right?

Pinner: Subject areas, yes.

Todd: When you reviewed the tape, were you reviewing it for some kind of subject matter?

Pinner: No, I've overheard it. I haven't personally sat down and listened to it myself. I just heard it being played.

Todd: Where did you hear it being played?

Pinner: In the courthouse.

Todd: Was that tape played for the benefit of Mr. Manuel before he testified?

Pinner: No.

Todd: Who was playing the tape with you in the courthouse?

Pinner: They were reviewing it in the deputy district attorney's office.

Todd: Who was present when it was reviewed?

Pinner: Myself, my partner, deputy district attorney Silverman. I don't remember who else.

Todd: Was Manuel present?

Pinner: No.

Todd: What was the date that you reviewed this tape?

Pinner: Today.

Todd: And the tape labeled 2 of 309790, did you ever review that tape?

Pinner: No.

Todd: Tape number 303881, a tape of Cecelia Amador. Did you review this tape?

Silverman: I'm going to object. Asked and answered.

The court: Overruled.

Pinner: No.

Todd: Tape number 302094 of Efrain Ortega, did you ever review that tape?

Pinner: No.

Todd: Tape 308789 of Alma Oseguera, O-S-E-G-U-E-R-A, did you ever review that tape?

Pinner: No.

Todd: Tape number 302095, did you ever review the tape of Ricardo Trujillo?

Pinner: No.

Todd: Tape number 308113, tape interview of Juan Catalan, did you ever review that tape?

Pinner: That one I can't remember.

Todd: Did you review the second tape interview of Ms. Amador, tape number 292949?

Pinner: No.

Todd: And I have four assorted tapes labeled 911 calls, radio calls, LAPD communication tapes and CHP 911. Did you review any of those tapes?

Pinner: Yes.

Todd: Which ones did you review?

Pinner: I remember reviewing the… I'm not saying it's all of it, but the CHP 911 and parts and portions of the LAPD 911.

Todd: Which, if anything, did you determine was significant or relevant to this case from reviewing those tapes?

Pinner: It's probably all significant and relevant.

Todd: What is it that you learned?

Pinner: Related to the CHP 911 tape, I listened to… boy, at least one phone call that I remember from a man identifying himself as Raymond speaking about the shooting and seeing people running around and things like that.

Todd: Anything else that you reviewed that was significant and relevant?

The court: That's an overbroad question. I'm going to sustain the court's own objection.

Todd: Did you write a report with regard to what you learned off this tape? You didn't do a follow-up or supplemental report or anything in that regard?

Pinner: I got a little lost in the question. It was a little too many questions at once.

Todd: You ever do a supplemental report based upon what you learned in the tapes that you reviewed?

Pinner: Not a supplemental report, no.

Todd: Did you make any kind of written notations regarding what you heard in the tapes?

Pinner: No, not specifically like language and things like that, no.

Todd: Did you ever discuss what Ms. Amador said about the incident on may 12th with detective Shaw?

Pinner: Can I have that one more time please?

Todd: Sure. Did you ever discuss with detective Shaw what Cecelia Amador said about what happened on the night of the shooting?

Pinner: Yes.

Todd: Did he go over with you everything that she talked about in her interview?

Pinner: No.

Todd: What did you learn from the interview of detective Shaw regarding Cecelia Amador?

Silverman: I'm going to object. Cumulative.

The court: Sustained.

Todd: On the grounds, your Honor?

The court: Well, I'm going to sustain it on the grounds that it's overbroad. Again, asking what he learned. I'm going to ask that you rephrase your question please.

Todd: Did you get a witness description from Cecelia Amador regarding the shooter, where she learned it, from any source?
Silverman: Well, I'm going to object, your Honor. That would call for double hearsay.

Todd: Prop 115, your Honor.

The court: Overruled subject to a motion to strike. You may answer the question.

Pinner: I'm aware of it by visually reading a report, sorry, notes, and the report prepared by detective Shaw of Cecelia's interview which is, you know, part of her interview of those days, and I'm aware of her description, based on her memory of what Manuel told her what he saw and heard at the crime scene.

Todd: Do you recall from the notes, or your interviews with detective Shaw regarding Ms. Amador, that Martha and Cecelia had been arguing which was overheard in a phone conversation?

Silverman: Well, I'm going to object. That's compound.

The court: Sustained.

Todd: Did you determine, or learn through your interview of Detective Shaw, and or the notes of the interview, that Martha was present with Cecelia and Ricardo and Manuel while Martha was on the phone with Efrain Ortega?

Silverman: Same objection.

The court: Sustained.

Todd: Did you learn from your conversation with detective Shaw, from the notes of the interview, that Cecelia, Manuel, Ricardo Trujillo and Roberto Marquez drove over to Martha's house?

Pinner: I don't believe that I can say that I learned that from the notes.

Todd: Did you learn that from somewhere?

Pinner: Yes.

Todd: Where did you learn it from?

Pinner: I suppose I came to that conclusion based

on multiple discussions with multiple detectives, based on their interviews of multiple witnesses, that those are the people that were there.

Todd: Based upon your review of the evidence in this matter, isn't it true that Roberto Marquez drove Manuel, Ricardo Trujillo and Cecelia Amador over to Martha's house?
Silverman: Well, I'm going to object based on the form of the question, unless it's based on an interview.

Todd: I also ask that the detective not keep looking to the D.A.

The court: Well, he can look anywhere he wants. It is calling for multiple layers of hearsay, and it's cumulative. Sustained.

Todd: Did you learn from the interview of Cecelia Amador that she saw a black Camry driving by about four times and slowly?

Silverman: Your Honor, based on the detective's earlier statement that he didn't interview her, it's multiple hearsay.

The court: Sustained.

Todd: Did you learn from detective Shaw, or from your review of the notes in this case of the interview of Cecelia Amador, that she saw a Black Camry driving by about four times and slowly?

Silverman: Same objection.

The court: Sustained.

Todd: On the grounds, your Honor?

The court: Multiple layers of hearsay.

Todd: Is detective Shaw on vacation?

Pinner: No, sir.

Todd: Did you interview Julio Juarez?

The court: Do you need…

Todd: J-u-l-i-o; Juarez, J-u-a-r-e-z.

Pinner: I don't know.

Todd: Would you like to review your notes?

Pinner: Please.

Todd: Please do.

The court: Can you direct him?

Todd: My murder book is in different sections than his. For your reference, he was the boss of Mr. Manuel.

Pinner: No. I have the interview in front of me. I believe I was involved in part of that interview.

Todd: Who else was involved in the interview?

Pinner: My partner, detective Rodriguez.

Todd: Did you determine the cell phone number that belongs to Julio Juarez?

Pinner: My notes don't indicate what his cell phone number is… or sorry that's… actually, I need to correct myself there. My partner's notes don't indicate what Mr. Juarez's…

Todd: Well, let me ask…

The court: Well, let him complete his sentence.

Pinner: My partner's notes and my notes don't indicate what Julio Juarez's cell phone number is.

Todd: Mind if I approach and look at your notes?

Pinner: Sure.

Todd: Did you, at some point, determine the phone number that was used, or the cell phone number that was used my Manuel on the night of May 12th?

Pinner: Yes.

Todd: What number is that?

Pinner: (XXX) XXX… I have to check the rest of it in my notes.

Todd: Would it be XXXX?

Pinner: Yes.

Todd: Did you learn where Manuel got this particular phone?

Pinner: Yes.

Todd: Where did he get the phone from?

Pinner: From his boss, Mr. Juarez.

Todd: And did Manuel have permission to have the phone on that night on May 12th?

Pinner: I assume so, yes.

Silverman: Well, based on that, I am going to object. It calls for speculation and move to strike.

The court: Yes, sustained. Be stricken.

Todd: Isn't it true that Mr. Juarez said that he gave the phone to Mr. Manuel, that he usually keeps it over the weekends, and he gives it back afterwards?

Pinner: Yes.

Todd: Did you get the cell phone records for that cell phone number?

Pinner: Yes.
Todd: And how did you get the cell records?

Pinner: From you.

Todd: Did you ever get them during your investigation?

Silverman: Well, your Honor, if that includes what he got in the defense, I think the answer is…

The court: Well, he is hesitating. Are you having trouble answering that question?

Pinner: Yes, you Honor.

The court: Do you want to rephrase it.

Todd: Did you ever get the cell phone records for that phone number before you got them from me?

Silverman: I am going to object. Calls for discovery and irrelevant according to counsel's own motion.

The court: Sustained.

Todd: Your honor, I believe that it would go to his course of investigation and how he determined time lines, and things of that nature, about when the crime happened.

The court: Well, how he went about establishing the time line. What relevance would that be?

Todd: I'm assuming that he's a detective and investigating this murder and trying to piece together facts, statements and time lines.

The court: But how he pieced it together would be irrelevant. It's how it's pieced together.

Todd: Well I'm asking him.

The court: All right. Ask another question.

Todd: So you did not obtain cell records from this phone number prior to getting them from me; is that correct?

Silverman: Same objection, your honor. It's irrelevant.

The court: Sustained.

Todd: After you got the phone records from myself, did you determine that Manuel had called Martha on the night of May 12th?

Pinner: No.

Todd: I'm sorry?

Pinner: No.

Todd: Did you ever review the phone records that were given to you by me?

Pinner: Yes.

Todd: And did Manuel's cell phone call Martha's?

Pinner: I don't think so.

Todd: Why do you believe that?

Pinner: I believe Martha called Manuel's phone. That was my interpretation of the records.
Todd: Well, you were here when the representative of the cell phone company testified, were you not?
Pinner: Yes.

Todd: And were you not present for the testimony when he said that the phone number XXX-XXXX called

XXX-XXXX.

Silverman: Well, I'm going to object. That speaks for itself. The opinion of this detective is irrelevant.

The court: Well, you can ask whether… he can ask whether he heard that testimony.

Pinner: I heard parts of that testimony, your honor. I just don't specifically recall that sentence or those sentences.

The court: Okay.

Todd: Showing you exhibit "F." Do you remember seeing this document previously?

Pinner: Yes.

Todd: At 10:02:07 on May 12th, 2003, the mobile number XXX-XXXX called XXX-XXXX for a call that lasted 30 seconds.

Pinner: I just disagree with that interpretation.

Todd: Why do you disagree with that interpretation?

Pinner: Because this column… there are eight columns in this chart that is marked as defense exhibit "F," and on line 4, at 22:02 on May 12th, I interpreted this to be that the phone number, the cell phone number that Manuel had, the XXX number, received a call under the calling number column from Martha's phone.

Todd: So when the custodian of records testified that the dialed number was the phone that was doing the dialing, and the calling number was a number that it was connected to, that person would have been in error; is that correct?

Silverman: I'm going to object. That calls for a conclusion.

The court: Sustained.

Todd: Your honor, he has testified that he is… directly testified in opposite to what the custodian of records testified.

The court: His opinion of whether the custodian is in error is irrelevant. His opinion of what someone else's testimony is would be irrelevant.

Even though this happened 20 years ago, it still brings me feelings of anger, frustration, and helplessness. When we are young children, we are taught that the police and high-ranking officials are the good people, which for the most part I do believe. However, cases like mine—and thousands of others—are a different story. It is demoralizing to think of the fundamental creed of the United States, "Liberty and justice for all." Now put yourselves in my place and tell me how you would feel.

Perhaps the toughest testimony I watched was when Melissa took the stand. Todd mentioned he might possibly call Melissa as a crucial witness, but we didn't think it was probable, considering that she was only five years old. Out of frustration, my mom would repeat over and over, "Melissa, why can't you be older so you could testify for your dad?"

As Alma thought about it, she recalled the movie Big Daddy, starring Adam Sandler. In the movie, the costar, Julian, who was only a child, had to testify on Sonny's (Sandler) behalf. Alma explained to Melissa that she needed to do the same for me.

Melissa was called to the stand and did amazing! Watching her, though, a wave of rage overcame me, because their incompetence not only affected me—my family was now being dragged through the mud! In the documentary, I'm shown breaking down during her testimony because I felt that her innocence was on trial.

Melissa answered every question that Todd asked her truthfully. When he was done, the judge asked Silverman if she wanted to cross examine her, and she declined. In hindsight, I wish she would have; if would have made Silverman look worse since very young children do not lie, unlike grown so-called professionals.

When the closing statements began, they all began to speak legal jargon. The DA was pushing for trial. Todd was arguing that the evidence pointed in my favor and showed that I had not been the shooter.

"Your honor," Todd closed, "it's by the Grace of God that Juan received tickets the morning of the day for that game; otherwise, the DA would have him heading straight to death row for something they have no evidence of."

Then there was more legal talk. Some of it I understood, most of it I didn't. I was confused and scared to think that I was headed straight to death row.

With the evidence presented and the closing arguments heard, Judge Dunn was about to make her ruling.

Even though the courtroom was filled beyond capacity, The room was quiet. The pounding of my heart, though, was deafening.

Here is Judge Dunn's ruling verbatim:

```
All right.

    Well, let me just briefly respond, since this
has been a lengthy preliminary hearing.
As you both have indicated, the people's case
rests solely on the eyewitness testimony of one
individual. I don't have any doubt that Manuel,
that eyewitness, attempted to be credible, but
he observed this murder on a dark residential
street, under, obviously, the most traumatic of
circumstances.

    When he is given the first opportunity to
make an identification, he selects two persons who
bear no resemblance, or very little resemblance, to
the defendant.

    It appears to me that the composite is the
strongest evidence that the people have, but the
making of a composite, in and of itself, is highly
unreliable.
```

Todd leaned over and whispered in my ear, "It's over."

Based upon the testimony, the defendant, Juan Catalan, has very little motive, had very little motive, if any, for an execution-style murder.

Based upon the testimony he's not a gang member. He was not driving the car that was described, the chevy malibu. He doesn't match the physical description of being 5' 8" and chubby. He's not wearing the clothing that was described.
During the interrogation, which I did listen to, he was told by the detectives that he had been - that his photo had been selected by multiple witnesses. During that interview he begs for a polygraph.

When asked by the detectives about his whereabouts on the night of the murder, he kept saying that he didn't know because he didn't know when the murder had occurred. It seems to me to be a reasonable inference that had he committed the murder, he would have known that he did so on the way home from a Dodger game, and he would have offered that alibi to the detectives during that interrogation.

The detective testified that this murder occurred somewhere between 10:00 and 10:30. The defendant makes a call and there is ample testimony that he was at Dodger Stadium at 10:11.
Based upon the People's case, aside from the alibi, I do not have any suspicion that the defendant committed this crime, and this case is dismissed.

In a movie, the next scene would be the front doors of the LA County Jail opening wide and me stepping out to meet my family. But this didn't happen. The preliminary trial ended around 1:00 p.m. It would normally take 60 minutes at most to file the paperwork necessary to release me, as the goal is to make sure this is done by 6:00 p.m., which is the last release of the day.

I was released on January 6th at 5:59 p.m.—not kidding here, exactly 5:59 p.m.

The LAPD wanted to hold me as long as was legally possible, so one minute before 6:00 p.m., I walked out the door a free man.

My family was waiting for me, and the first person I hugged was Melissa since she had been the saddest since the day I was arrested. And just like the day she was born, I did not want to let her go. Then I hugged the rest of my family. And when I got to Todd. I not only hugged him, I picked him up.

"I owe you everything," I said, trying to hold the tears back.

Todd smiled and stayed with my family for a few minutes, then I turned around and noticed he was no longer there.
Gone. Like Batman.

"So," Alma asked through a beaming smile, "where do you want to eat? We'll get you anything you want."

My answer was not something to eat, but rather something to drink— something I had been craving for the six months I was inside.

"A Coke," I said.

We stopped at a Carl's Jr. and got my Coke, then headed to pick up Mariah at daycare. When I walked in the door, Mariah was the only kid left. Her back was turned to us, so she never saw me walk in. I paused and silently watched her play for a minute. The two ladies who ran the daycare had been following my case on TV, and when one of them saw me, she covered her mouth with both hands, as if in shock. I smiled at her, still keeping my eyes on Mariah.

Walking across the room, I stood behind Mariah and tapped her on the shoulder. When she saw me, she smiled and said the sweetest thing I've ever heard. "Dad," she said softly.

I am in tears while writing this; it was a beautiful moment I will never forget.
Thank you, God.

*PA Announcer: Ladies and gentlemen, it's time for the 7th inning stretch, accompanied by Nancy Bea at the Dodger Stadium rolling organ, let's all sing "Take me out to the ballgame." *Crowd sings along*
4-3 Atlanta bottom of the seventh inning. Ron Coomer will bat for Hideo Nomo, and Jung Keun Bong takes over on the mound. By the way, his middle name, Keun (K-E-U-N), he added it because he says that people back home in South Korea liked players with three names. Like the Cub's first baseman, Hee-Seop Choi. So, Jung Keun Bong is a highly touted pitcher in Korea. He's from Seoul. His mom, and well his parents and one of his three sisters still live in Seoul, and what he did, he moved to Norcross, Georgia and did not go home. He only goes now back to Korea maybe one month a year.*

He speaks English very well; he learned it while living in Norcross. And now here's Coomer to challenge him. Ball one, 1 and 0. So, Ron Coomer off the bench trying to get Izturis home. 4-3 Atlanta. The Dodgers have trailed 1-0, 2-1, 3-1, 3-2, and now 4-3. Ground foul over the head of Glenn Hoffman, one and one. Jung Keun Bong facing Ron Coomer, bottom of the seventh. Bong is 6'3" and 180. He is 22 years old; he'll be 23 the middle of July. They say that because of the unrest with North Korea that he calls his family almost every day. FASTBALL WHACKED INTO CENTER! HERE COMES ANDRUW JONES, HERE COMES CESAR IZTURIS, HE'S IN THERE, AND THE DODGERS HAVE TIED IT UP! And Ron Coomer goes Bing Bong, and the Dodgers are even.

Vin Scully, Dodger's Stadium, May 12, 2003

CHAPTER EIGHT

School Daze

*S*o one away and Javy Lopez coming up. So the veteran catcher who is hitting .255. Last year, he had a career batting average going in at .287, but he hit only .233. So that was an off year for sure. Now LoDuca going out to talk, so that'll give us time. Lopez two for nine against Quantrill, that's a .222 batting average. Awe, there's a picture. Happy father with two youngsters taking in the game. Tomorrow night, Ortiz and Ishii; Wednesday night, Greg Maddux and Kevin Brown. Breeze picking up a little bit, blowing out to right field. One out eighth inning 4-4, 3-2 Montreal in the eighth inning up at PacBell. Ball one. Andres Galarraga had a key base hit to drive in one, and then Vladimir Guerrero threw what would've been the tying run out at the plate. So, Montreal still leading 3-2. Now they're heading to the ninth inning up north, meanwhile Quantrill behind 2 and 0 and Vinny Castilla on deck. Jones at first, chopper to the hole. GREAT STOP BY IZTURIS AND THEY GET A DOUBLE PLAY! Is that kid something special, WOW! Cesar Izturis gets fives going into the dugout as he flashes to his right off balance throw to Alex, who clears the way easily to double him up. And at the end of seven and a half, a 4-4 tie.

Vin Scully, Dodger's Stadium, May 12, 2003

I was FINALLY out, but I would soon be back in.

The court had 'lost" my release papers on the drug case, which meant that I had to get rebooked and released.

"What?" I asked Todd, thinking this had to be a joke.

"Juan, I'm sorry, but you'll be you out between 24 to 48 hours max."

It wasn't a joke.

I was released on a Tuesday, found out I had to be rebooked the day after, on Wednesday, and they wanted me to turn myself in on Thursday.

"Monday," I said. "Alma is taking me to Las Vegas for the weekend. Can we make Monday work?"

"Sure, go to Vegas, relax, have fun, and you'll turn yourself in on Monday."

So we went to Vegas, and as much as I tried to celebrate and enjoy the trip, I couldn't get my mind off the fact that I would be back in that shithole soon.

Monday arrived, along with a black cloud that hung over me. I was driven to the County and turned myself back in to get reprocessed. As I was waiting to get interviewed as a new inmate by the sheriffs, for the second time, I saw someone I knew from the neighborhood, Francisco Saldivar, better known as "Pancho." Now, for those who may not be aware of this, when you are in jail and you run into someone you know, it might—or might not—be a good thing.

Pancho turned when I called his name, and I walked over to shake the hand of the man I'd known for years. What I didn't know then (and wouldn't for some time) was that I was now shaking the hand of the informant against me—the one the police called "Mr. Sam." That's right, Pancho was the individual who led the police in my direction. I never saw him again.

When the processing interview was complete, I was taken to the 2000 floor, AGAIN, and guess what the very first thing I heard was. The alarm.

"What's going on?" I asked a Hispanic inmate walking by.

"Be on your toes, homie," he said. "They just killed two black inmates."

Fuck.

I had been away from the race politics of jail for a week, but here it was again.

I went to the dining hall to be taken to my cell, all while the alarm was blaring. But through the noise, I could still hear someone shout my name.

"CATALAN!" the deputy yelled. "Charlie Roe, cell 7," so I followed him. When we got to cell 7, there was a large black inmate standing in front of the cell, blocking it.

"You from 'Set' gang?" he asked, his arms folded across his chest.

"No," I answered. He moved to the side, and I walked in.

The cells held six men each, and there's supposed to be a mix of races to reduce racial tensions. In this cell, there were four blacks, one paisa, and me. And it just so happened that the two inmates that were just killed belonged to the same gang as the four guys in my cell.

Double fuck.

I was watched as I entered the cell, but not a word was spoken to me. The tension was as thick as L.A. smog when the paisa sat next to me.

"Qvo compa," he said softly, "Si algo pasa yo brinco contigo." Translated, he said, "What's up, my friend? If something happens, I'm with you." He knew exactly what was going on.

Todd's promise that I would be out of jail within only a few hours stretched into days. And each day was worse than the last. The tension in the cells was almost unbreathable, so much so that I couldn't sleep for more than a few minutes. These guys were planning and whispering in the corner, and I could barely make out what they were saying,

"Man, FUCK THAT. An eye for an eye!" one of them said.

"Man, he isn't even from that gang," another one said.

I listened and thought, I beat the murder case and was released, only to be sent back here to die?

I had nowhere to go, and no one was coming to help me. I just couldn't believe it had come to this. I remember thinking that I needed to say goodbye to my family, AGAIN!

I called my parents' house, and Alma happened to be over there visiting. I couldn't put my thoughts together, so I told her that I was leaving.

"Leaving?" she asked. "Leaving where?" I couldn't explain what was going on, so I just told her that I loved her and the kids.

You can tell in jail if you have been marked. I can't explain it, but you just know. And that night was the night. I knew it as soon as I saw a couple black trustees bring my cellmates some fresh linens. From the outside, this probably wouldn't mean anything. The problem wasn't the blankets, but what was inside the blankets. When I saw them, I knew that tonight my life would end.

Every day and every night, the inmates are counted to make sure everyone is there. But for some reason, there was a new deputy doing count, a black deputy I had never seen before. When he got to our cell, he looked inside and then paused for a second. He saw the four black inmates huddled in the corner, and then he saw me on the top right side bunk. Picking up on this, he looked at me and asked, "You alright in there?"

I wanted to say, hell no, but I couldn't do that.

"I'm good," I said, lying through my teeth.

"We all good in here, Sheriff," one of the inmates said.

But the deputy just looked back at me. "I don't believe you," he said. "Jump down from there."

So I did.

"Lift up your shirt and turn around." I did that, too, knowing that the deputy was checking for stab wounds.

He thought for a minute before announcing, "I'm getting you out of here."

I literally was saved from not one near-death experience, but TWO, in less than a week!

I was moved to a cell down the hall that housed a majority of Hispanics. Shit, I finally showered and got as good of a night's sleep as you can get in jail.

I am absolutely convinced that that deputy saved my life. And I never got his name.

Two weeks later, I was released.

***

I had to go to court one more time to finalize my requirements from the drug charges, and two things happened when I did. The first was that I told Todd a secret—my secret—the one that had been percolating in my head for a while and was now ready to come out.

"I'm going back to school," I told Todd.

"Juan, that's great," he said. And he even included this in his comments at the end of the court proceedings.

"Mr. Catalan," Judge Dunn said, "I congratulate you on going back to school, and I look forward to an invitation to your graduation."

Wait, did a judge really just say that to me? Having someone of her stature believe in me was both motivational and inspirational to me. I have never had that in my life. She then told me how I should carry my life from there on out. She said, "Mr. Catalan, there are going to be a lot of people that feel like you got away with murder. If I were you, I would live my life as best as I can and do not give anyone a reason to talk."

Being released the second time, the final time, created an indescribable mix of emotions. I was so grateful to be back with my family, and I was very grateful for this new chance.

And the judge's words echoed inside my head.

***

I started working with my dad in his shop again, and he was as happy as I'd ever seen him. But I also had to make good on the promise I had made to myself and God about going back to school. But that wasn't all—I also made two more promises. The second one was that I would go to the church I attended as a kid. From the sidewalk curb outside, I would get on my knees and, still on my knees, make my way to the front door. I did that. My last promise was that I would share God's love and the grace that I have experienced with the world. I have spoken about God's goodness on different platforms, but with this book, I hope that message reaches the entire planet.

Going back to school was an entirely different and new experience. I didn't know where to start, so I did some research and found that West Valley Occupational offered help to people in getting their G.E.D.

That week, I went to West Valley Occupational Center in Woodland Hills and signed up. Since that was my first goal, I needed to get that out of the way. With their help, I studied for about six months and signed up to take the G.E.D. test in Los Angeles College.

I passed the test on my first try. Then I walked across the street and enrolled into L.A Pierce College. Since I had been away from school for so long, I had to take an assessment test to see where I was academically. In math, I wasn't very good, so I started at the bottom, Math 110, I believe. For English, a little worse, I ended up starting one level above E.S.L. But I was determined to do this. I was going to be a college student.

I began attending Pierce College in the spring of 2005. Since I was only taking two courses a semester while working, it would be a long road, but I was okay with that. It's funny, when I was younger, I looked at classes as a waste of time. Now, I had a different perspective, always looking for what I could take from this.

At first, while attending school, I felt physically and mentally sick, which I took as a sign that I was overworked and taking too much on. I mean, there were times when I was attending school and working two jobs at the same time, so I thought I was just stressed out. But it didn't get better.

I went to see a doctor, who gave me a physical and ordered blood tests. Everything checked out okay, so my doctor just told me to take it easy. I tried, but it was easier said than done. They say that anxiety is the thief of joy and, man, could I relate to that. It's crazy to think something like anxiety can run in a family, but it seemed like this was the case. My brother and sisters have also dealt with this issue. On top of work and school, I had a pending lawsuit against the City of Los Angeles for the malice/incompetence of the LAPD.

I loved my classes in Health and Psychology (Parent-child relations). I learned so much information and gathered so many tools that I began to use in my parental life. I was learning the importance of communication with my kids. The English classes were enjoyable; it was as if I was learning to read and write for the first time.

The course was English 21, and the professor was Mr. Coonfield. If you want a visual of Mr. Coonfield, just picture Santa Claus teaching a college course. He was a good teacher, but, MAN, could he put the class to sleep when he lectured.

Our textbook for the course was titled The Least You Should Know

About English. One day, I was dozing in and out as Mr. Coonfield lectured. To stay awake, I started flipping through the book, going from page to page. Out of nowhere, I saw my name on a page in the textbook.

What! I felt like I levitated off my chair!

My heart started racing, and I looked around the room, convinced everyone knew who I was.

I read the piece about me.

"Going to a baseball game is fun. Not so for a particular man. Juan Catalan went to a baseball game with his girlfriend."

Well, I thought, I went to the game with my daughter, not my girlfriend.

The class took a break, and I lingered in the back, wrestling with my thoughts. After a few minutes, I finally get up and made my way to the front of the class, where Mr. Coonfield had his face down grading papers.

"Umm, excuse me, Mr. Coonfield?"

"Yeah, yeah what is it?" he grumbled.

"Umm, I think I found an error in the textbook."

Mr. Coonfield froze. "YOU found an error in the textbook?" He smirked and looked over to my book. "Where's the error?"

I pointed to the story.

"Here. I was with my daughter," I said, "not my girlfriend."

Confused, he grabbed my book, read it and looked at me. Then he looked back at the book and then back at me again.

"Hmm, well, what do you know? Your name is in here," he said in a snarky tone. "Why couldn't they have old Bill Coonfield in there?"

He handed me back my book and continued grading.

He thought I was joking.

In history, I was learning about those who came before us. Political Science and Philosophy helped me begin to think critically. In Economics, I learned that an economy is a living thing. All of it was amazing. Except--.

Math had never been my thing, And I'm not afraid to admit that. Back in high school, I struggled with algebra, so it didn't come as a surprise that my college math classes were more difficult, which meant I struggled more.

When I talked with Todd about college, I always told him that I was struggling with the math part.

Todd would smile and slap my back. "I only like counting hundreds."

But my favorite class in college? Ready? Theatre. I had so much fun learning about what actors go through and learning what it takes to play a convincing role.

I graduated with an associate's degree in general education from Pierce College in 2012. I was so happy that day to have my parents and my family in attendance. I felt like that was my first real accomplishment in my life—besides being a dad. But I wanted to take my education further.

I transferred to Los Angeles Valley College to complete the rest of my lower division classes, and I took my final community college courses online during the Pandemic. Then, I applied to Cal State University of Northridge.

I was accepted.

When I got the acceptance letter, I had to let it sink in for a moment. From never graduating high school to now receiving an acceptance letter to Cal State University of Northridge, how crazy is that?

"You can do anything, if you put your mind to it," I told Melissa and Mariah, waving the acceptance letter in the air. "Any—thing!"

So at 44 years old, I began attending Cal State Northridge.

Attending the university at 44 is defiantly different than it is for those in their 20's. But then I realized that being in your 20's is just a different mindset. A different trajectory.

The 20-year-old college student doesn't have a clue what they want to do with their life—and that's fine. They have plenty of time to figure that out. But us old guys—we are on a path and have a clearer goal in mind.

A lot of the coursework revolves around group work, I think to simulate the real world and how to deal with many people. The problem is trying to find common ground with 20-year-old students, a majority of whom are know it alls. The first group I had was in my Gateway 302 class. It was difficult to say the least, but I managed.

Being that we have the family business I have often thought I could use my degree to grow the business or to open up a new business or two.

On the first day of school, I was beyond nervous when I walked into my first class, surrounded by kids in their 20's. Immediately, I felt out of place and uncomfortable. Just like back in elementary school, I was the odd kid out.

I start out every semester focused on doing well in the class, being there, taking notes. When I am in school and, of course, working at the same time, it takes a heavy toll on me, and my stress and anxiety levels skyrocket. I have been through insomnia, facial rashes, and even hair loss because of all the stress. On top of that, I am seemingly in a bad mood all the time, which my family hates. When this happens, I have to remind myself why I'm doing this.

And—how far I have come.

Thinking about that centers me.

One time, I was in a university hall and it hit me. I never graduated high school. I've done jail time. I was accused of a heinous crime that I did not commit. And now, I'm not only at one of the reputable universities in the country—but I am excelling there.

I struggled but I did well. The thing that makes me prouder is the thought that even though I have struggled with college, it is the opposite for my daughters, Melissa and Mariah. Whenever I think they are struggling, you can understand my joy when I ask them about their grades and their responses are "A's" and "B's."

What I learned in my first year at the university was that being a professional is hard! You must pay attention to details because it can be the difference in things going your way or losing an opportunity. I ended up getting a B in both of my first two classes, which to me is equivalent to getting A's.

"You know, Juan," one of my teachers told me, "you might want to consider journalism."

A little confused, I smiled. "Journalism? Why?"

He held up the paper I had turned in. "I like the writing. You tell the story well."

And since you are reading this book, I guess he was right.

I was released in the beginning of 2004, and even though Todd had endured the film crew recording my court proceedings when I got out, I never wanted to stand in front of a camera again. I wanted to erase the events from that time period from my memory, delete it, and live as if it never happened. Most of all, I just wanted to be with my family and to work and learn. And I was able to do that for about five months after my release.

That is, until an article about me came out in The New Yorker.

That—changed —everything.

"Want to go to New York?" Todd asked me over the phone.

"New York?" I asked. "For what?"

"Good Morning America wants to fly you, Alma, and Melissa there."

"No."

I tried to reason that I didn't want to be interviewed, which was true, but there was also the fact that I had a fear of flying. I hadn't been on a plane in 15 years! Todd is a smart guy and figured that out quickly.

"You're getting on that plane."

"Oh yeah?" I laughed. "How are you doing that?"

"Because I'm going with you."

And he did. Good Morning America booked the four of us on the same plane. But before I got on that flight, I took some Nyquil and slammed a shot of tequila. That's how I survived the flight.

With the flight behind me, I was excited to be in New York for the first time.

We arrived safely, and while walking through JFK Airport, we saw a limo driver with a card that read "Catalan."
"Oh, wow," I told Alma, pointing to the card. "Someone with my last name gets to ride in a limo."

Alma stopped and looked at me in disbelief. Then I got it. They were there for us.

We got in the limo around 6:00 a.m., and we had to do Good Morning America at 7 a.m.! Once we were driven to Times Square to the famous "Millennium Hotel," we literally had 15 minutes to freshen up before walking across the street to the ABC Studios.

As we did, Todd's said something that stopped me.

"You know that ten million people will be watching you live."

"Live? Wait, they don't—they don't tape these things?"

"They do, but not this one. You will be with Diane Sawyer and Charlie Gibson live."

Melissa took my hand, and she was interviewed with me, being her super adorable self.

Todd wanted to get the most TV exposure for our story. So when we left GMA, we made our way over to NBC Studios, where we were interviewed on The Today Show with Katie Couric and Matt Lauer. After The Today Show, we made our way over to the Fox News Channel and did Linda Vester's live audience show, which was a shock to me. Then we went to ESPN, MSN, NBC News, and Telemundo. It was a whirlwind, for sure.

When we were inside the NBC Studios, we were in a show called "Access Hollywood." The coolest part of this interview was that at the end, they asked the tv audience if they thought that Larry David should invite me on Curb your Enthusiasm and have me on for a cameo! I'm still up for it, Larry, if you'll have me!

After TV, we did radio interviews. And when those were done, Todd called me.

"How do you feel?" he asked.

"Exhausted."

"Well, you have time for a nap, because there is more coming."

When I woke up, I really didn't want to do anymore interviews.

"Unless—" I said with a smile.

"Okay, sounds like we're negotiating. What are the terms?"

"Being a huge sports fan and being in the Big Apple, I want to go to a Yankee game."

Todd laughed. "Done," he said. "I'll set it up."

We were headed to our last interview, which was Court TV with Catherine Crier, who was also an ex-judge. For the most part, all the interviews consisted of the same questions with me providing the same answers. But there was one thing Catherine told me toward the end of the interview that really stayed with me.

She told me, "Well, Mr. Catalan, it looks like you have some very important things yet to do here on earth."

I listened and let that thought bounce around inside of my head for a while, then responded.

"Yeah," I said. "I guess I do."

We wrapped up the Court TV interview and headed to the Bronx. I asked if we could ride the subway to get the true NY experience, and Todd agreed. When we were riding on the subway, random people started recognizing us from the earlier TV interviews. Not kidding, that really happened. Todd and I even took pictures with the people who asked, which I thought was pretty cool. But it was the last interaction that blew me away.

Just as we were exiting the subway, a man walked up to me.

"Eres tu, eres tu de la tele," he said as he shook and held my hand, with Todd standing nearby, watching the interaction.

Then the man smiled and said, "Diosito nunca se olvida de la gente

Buena." I froze, and he walked away.

"What did he say?" Todd asked.

"It's you from the television. God never forgets about the good people," I replied.
"Wow," Todd said, placing his hand on my shoulder. "You'll never forget about that for the rest of your life,"

And he was right.

When we got to Yankee Stadium—and this was the old stadium (since then, I've actually been in both)—I bought tickets from a scalper. As we walked in, I was in instant awe! This was the house where Babe Ruth, Lou Gehrig, Joe DiMaggio, Yogi Berra, and Mickey Mantle once played! Once in our seats, I soaked it all in.

What a game it was! Kevin Brown, who was my favorite Dodger in the early 2000's had been traded to the Yankees after the 2003 season. I watched him dominate and be the ace of the Dodgers for about five years, and now I was watching him pitch at Yankee Stadium! I watched all time legends like "The Captain" Derek Jeter, "Arod" Alex Rodriguez, "Godzilla" Hideki Matsui, and "The Sandman" Mariano Rivera, who is the greatest closer ever to play! We saw eight total homeruns, and the Yankees won the game 7-6—again, what a game! The hot dogs at Yankee Stadium were two thumbs up, and I had my first ever slice of New York pizza, which was exactly as advertised.

Going to that game recharged my batteries, and I was able to focus again. We left the stadium and headed back to Times Square, where our hotel was, and the interviews continued the next day. We did interviews in Spanish, German, and Japanese. 60 Minutes reached out to us. In fact, after interviewing me, Rebecca from 60 Minutes gave us a personal NY tour. Then she took all of us, Todd included, out to a really nice dinner in Times Square. And Rebecca met us for an amazing breakfast at the famous "Plaza Hotel." My first trip to New York was absolutely surreal.

We all flew back to California, and I thought, great, that's done. But Todd had another surprise for me.

"I don't suppose you would have any interest in going to this with me, would you?" I felt something in my hand and looked down. It was not only Lakers tickets, but it was game two of the 2004 NBA Finals between the Lakers and Pistons.

I was wordless. I had never been to any kind of championship game, let alone a LAKER game! Even though the Lakers were the clear favorite to win the title, they had lost game one, so winning game two was crucial.

On Tuesday, June 8th, we drove to Staples Center, and I still couldn't believe I was going to watch the game live. Walking toward the main entrance, I noticed that Todd was veering off in another direction. To my surprise, we walked in through the VIP entrance, the one used by celebrities and professional athletes.

Again, I had to let it all sink in—Kobe, Shaq, Phil Jackson, and the greatness which was the Lakers. I saw Bill Russell, Kareem Abdul Jabbar, and Magic Johnson in attendance, among others. During halftime, we were walking around the concourse and ran into Lisa Leslie, who is arguably the greatest female player ever. She was super nice, and I took a picture with her—man, did I feel short standing next to her!

The game came down to the last 10 seconds, when who else but KOBE BRYANT hit a 3 pointer to tie the game—and Todd and I were sitting right behind the basket when Kobe hit the shot—to send the game into overtime. The Lakers dominated the overtime and won the game to tie the series, 1-1.

It was incredible, but the surprises that Todd had didn't stop there. He got us into Dr. Jerry Buss's "Chairman's Room," where all the stars hung out after the game. The next thing I knew, I was talking and having a drink with the Vice President of Pepsi North America at the bar. What happened next was almost like a dream. We had been down there for almost an hour when the door suddenly opened, and surrounded by four playmantes and his own security, who walked in, but none other than the legendary Laker's owner, Dr. Jerry Buss!

So, Todd started talking to his personal security guard, and the next thing I know, the guy headed over to Dr. Buss and whispered something in his ear. And what did Dr. Buss do? He stood up and waved us over! I almost passed out! I was SO shocked that the billionaire owner of the LAKERS was calling US over!

My mind drew a blank, and the only thing I could think to do was to extend my hand. Not only did Dr. Buss ignore my hand, but he proceeded to give me the biggest and most genuine hug I think I've ever had. After taking a few photos, he sat me down in his circle and asked questions. I think I answered them correctly, but to be honest, my mind had turned off by that time. I was speechless. Who wouldn't be?

There I was, sitting in front of the owner of the LOS ANGELES LAKERS, my favorite team on the planet, with four playmates all staring at me, probably wondering who the HELL I was. As I think back, I could've told Dr. Buss so many things—like it was my dream as a kid to play for the Lakers, or that Magic Johnson and Kobe Bryant were my all-time sports idols. I could have asked him how it felt to own the greatest team on the planet. I could have asked him if I could see the Lakers locker room or if I could get his autograph. But I didn't do any of that. No, I just smiled and nodded and believed that I answered a few questions correctly.

But while I forgot to do all that, I won't ever forget one thing that happened.

Dr. Buss smiled and pointed at me. "You got a win in court." Then he pointed at himself. "I got a win on the court."

WOW.

After that, I got to walk onto center court at Staples Center!

I will never be able to repay Todd for everything he's done for me—in court or otherwise.

Never.

***

That July, Todd called me.

"Do you know a Don Francisco?"

"Are you kidding me?" I laughed.

Don Francisco is a global icon that Latin people around the world follow. When I grew up, my parents tuned in to watch him on Saturdays and listen to his shenanigans, games, and guest stars, all wrapped up in one show. To people who are not familiar with Don Francisco, the best way to describe him is as The Spanish Oprah Winfrey, but he's kind of a goofball, as well.

Don Francisco's show had called and wanted to fly me out and put me up in Miami for a week. When I told my parents, they could not believe it. After not travelling outside of California for 15-plus years, I had been to New York and was now headed to Miami.

They flew Todd and me out, and we got the VIP treatment once again. I did the show and met the Mexican celebrities that I had watched when I was a kid. It was the greatest thing ever! I even had dinner with model Mayra Veronica of Don Francisco! All my family and friends watched, and soon my parents' phone was ringing.

***

When it came time to decide If I wanted to file a lawsuit against the City of Los Angeles for false imprisonment, I wasn't sure. That was a difficult decision to make. For one thing, I wanted to put this all behind me. I didn't want to relive the trauma of going through the murder case. Hearing all the negative voices in my head, I realized it came down to doing the easy thing, or the right thing. And the right thing was to make sure that justice was done.

So I now had work, school, my family, a large civil lawsuit, and my brother's case to deal with.

Mario's court case took a heavy toll on all of us, especially my parents. At one point, I couldn't help but think about my mom and what she must've felt with both of her sons fighting murder charges. just wow.

But as I mentioned, the one constant throughout my trials and tribulations has always been sports. Through all the ups and downs, sports have always been there to take my mind off of things. If you were to ask my family what sports do to me, they would say that all sports make me more stressed, but I say sports without passion is like peanut butter without jelly. They go together. One reason why I love sports so much is the passion that fans bring to the game. There's nothing like a walk-off homerun, or a buzzer-beating basket, or a game-winning touchdown with no time on the clock! The adrenalin fires you up, and you better bring the DAMN noise!

Any chance I got, of course, I would go to a Dodger's game, and Todd invited me all the time to Laker games. I was blessed to see Kobe in the prime of his career. The Dodgers weren't so good during the early to mid-2000's, but the Lakers were winning championships. Sports are like therapy to me. It's weird how a game can instantly lift me up and cheer me up when nothing else will. When my favorite football team, the 49ers, win a game, I'm feeling fantastic … at least, until the next game, haha!

Thanks to Todd, I was able to witness so many incredible moments. One of the most memorable sports games I've ever been to was the Lakers vs. Mavericks (December 20, 2005). Christmas was five days away, and Todd called and asked if I wanted to go. Like really, Todd?

Never in my wildest dreams would I imagine what I would witness on the court at that game and, especially, what happened after the game.

During the game, we witnessed Kobe Bryant take over the game, as he usually would, but in this game, he outscored the entire Dallas Mavericks team 61 points to 60 points after 3 quarters! The crowd was buzzing and in awe. Phil Jackson held Kobe out of the 4th quarter because the game was a blowout and well in hand. If he hadn't, many sports analysts think he might have scored more than 81 points, which is his all-time career high! I couldn't wait to go into the Chairman's Room after the game to see how all the fans would react to what we had just watched.

Todd brought along two basketballs to this game. When I asked him what the balls were for, he said that he would be traveling to Germany soon to visit his good friend, Jurgen, who had two sons that were HUGE Dirk Nowitzki fans. He was going to try and get them signed.

On our way underground, with the visiting team making their way to the locker room, Todd caught up to Mark Cuban, the billionaire owner of the Mavericks. He asked if there was any chance of getting Dirk to sign them.

"Dirk just lost, "Cuban said. "He's not in a good mood."

So we made our way into the Chairman's Room and joined in what was a historic night for Kobe and Laker Nation. Everyone was talking about nothing else but KOBE. All along, Todd was hoping to see Dirk come out of the visiting locker room, which was right outside the Chairman's Room. But no luck.

It was now a little past 11 p.m., and, having lost hope, Todd said let's go home. As we headed to the exit, Now, Todd knew the ins and outs of Staples Center, and as we headed out, he motioned for me to keep walking past the exit. We made our way into what was the players' parking lot, and as we came around the tunnel, we saw the Dallas Mavericks team bus.

Todd's crazy ass said he was going to look for Dirk.

"What?" I asked, shocked. The first thought that crossed my mind was that we were going to jail, especially when Todd walked over and went inside the bus! Now, over the years, I came up with a nickname for him ..."Fucking Todd," but it was a term of endearment! Just when I thought I had seen it all, he constantly outdoes himself! Anyhow, my back was against the wall in this hallway, and I was sweating bullets. I looked to the left and saw two shadows coming. Oh shit! But then my jaw dropped.

Meeting your real-life hero in person is a feeling we should all experience, at least once in our lifetime, but to meet multiple heroes is unexplainable! Coming out of the shadows was none other than Kobe Bryant, and he was walking straight toward me! At that point, my mind was blank, and I completely forgot about Todd and my fear of going to jail.

The moment Kobe walked right in front of me, I managed to say, "Kobeeeeeeee," and he looked at me.

"What's up, man?" he smiled.

"Can I get a picture?" I asked.

"Sure."

Within a matter of seconds, I was completely surrounded by what us Laker fans know as the "Red Coats," the security guards at Staples Center. They instantly start interrogating me.

"Who are you? How did you get down here?" Not knowing what to say, I showed them my Chairman's Room pass. One of the guys looked at it, and within another matter of seconds, a supervisor arrived, demanding an explanation. The person I gave my pass to said, "He has a pass."

During this whole time, Todd was on the Mavericks bus but must have noticed that Kobe was in front of me. Forgetting Dirk, he ran over and handed Kobe a ball to sign. Kobe stares at him for a second and then surprised us when he grabbed the ball and signed it! All the while, I was yelling at Todd to take a picture of me and Kobe. Being starstruck, Todd ignored me, so I screamed at the top of my lungs.

"TODD!" He snapped out of it, and I handed him my camera to take the picture. To this day, nearly everyone who sees that photo tells me they've NEVER seen me smile bigger!

As soon as we took the picture, Todd proceeded to hand Kobe the other ball. Looking at it, Kobe said, "Man, I can't be signing all that shit!" Todd was taken aback, and I chuckled. Kobe then walked off toward what I assumed was his Ferrari and drove off into the sunset. As we left Staples Center, I told Todd that I was now able to die in peace!

Of course, Todd would call me the next morning,

"You still alive?"

Bottom of the eighth inning in a 4-4 tie. He's got a little megaphone as Shawn Green checks in. Or either that is going to protect his arm when he's hitting. Shawn has walked twice and robbed of a possible homerun by Andruw Jones takes a hook for a strike, 0 and 1. Well, when the game started, we were talking about one of the attractions of the Atlanta Dodgers series, the prospects of the two great relievers, Eric Gagne and John Smoltz going head-to-head. Bobby Cox has used Reynolds, King, Hodges, and Bong. Meanwhile, Eric Gagne begins to loosen up for the ninth inning. Smoltz not up yet. Not yet. 0 and 1. Shawn hitting .278. Outside corner at the knees, big pitch, 0 and 2. Jung Keun Bong from Seoul, Korea. Now that slurve, one and two. Cesar Izturis used his head running, turned a single into a double and scored the tying run, made a dazzling stop of that ball hit by Lopez and turned into a double play. Little guys are sure fun to watch. Cora and Izturis, Furcal and Giles. So after that breaking ball down and away tried to come in on the hands and missed. Two and two. Shawn Green

doing pretty well against left handers hitting .347 against them this year.
Two and two. And got him on a breaking ball.

Vin Scully, Dodger's Stadium, May 12, 2003

CHAPTER NINE

Kobe

*W*hen the Dodgers come up in the bottom of the ninth inning, Beltre, Izturis, and Cabrera. With a four-run lead, you wonder if Bobby Cox will bring in John Smoltz, and John is still throwing down in the bullpen. Bobby talking to his pitching coach, Leo Mazone. Bong remember is still in the game; they didn't bat for him, he sacrificed. So Javy Lopez the ninth man to come up in the inning. Jung Keun Bong is the pitcher of record, and Brohawn trying to get an out and end the ninth. Two out up north and it's still four 4-3 in favor of Montreal. Jose Cruz Jr. just struck out for the second out; meanwhile, a drive that's gonna carry into the seats, and this game is just completely crumbled. As Troy Brohawn gives up a three-run homerun to Javy Lopez. So the Dodgers shining moment, the bullpen has had a bad night. It is 11-4 Atlanta. They've scored seven times in the ninth inning. They had four runs against Nomo, but then broke it open with four against Gagne and now three against Brohawn.

Vin Scully, Dodger's Stadium, May 12, 2003

Christmas came, and I made it to Todd's house to exchange a few gifts and watch the Lakers play Shaq and the Miami Heat. At halftime, Todd handed me my present. I should've known it was going to be a WOW moment when Todd brought out his camcorder and started recording.

The red light on the recorder turned on, and I smiled and began to tear the wrapping paper off the box. Right away, I saw the orange leather of a basketball. When the rest of the paper came off, I saw it—an official NBA basketball in its case! I was so excited because I never had an official NBA ball.

"Wow, Todd," I said. "Thank you so much, this is—."

But Todd just shook his head. "You opened it the wrong way," he smiled. "Turn it around."

When I did, I saw a signature on the part of the ball memorabilia collectors call the sweet spot.

Kobe Bryant.

"What?!" I screamed.

Todd then told me that he'd asked for a personal favor from Bob Steiner, Dr. Buss's right-hand man, who had Kobe sign the basketball the night we were at the Mavericks game!"

"No way, how?" I asked.
Smiling, Todd told me the story.

After he graduated from law school, Todd started his career as a Deputy D.A. One of the first cases he tried was a young man in his early 20's, who had a recurring drug abuse problem which led to multiple arrests. Usually, he would have been booked with this same charge and would be sentenced to jail time. But this time, it was Todd's recommendation that the district attorney's office send this young man to a rehabilitation center, instead. The defendant's counsel agreed, and so did the judge.

As Todd was getting ready to leave the courtroom, a gentleman approached him.

"Hello," he said. "My name is Bob Steiner, and I am that young man's father. I just wanted to thank you for not sending my son to jail but rather try to get him some help."

"You're welcome," said Todd, shaking the man's hand. "I hope he can turn a corner from all of this."

As Todd turned to walk away, Steiner stopped him.

"Listen," said Steiner. "I don't know if you like basketball, but I work for the Los Angeles Lakers, and if you ever want to come to a game, just give me a call." He gave Todd his business card and left.

Todd took him up on that offer, and the two became friends. Todd's good-hearted compassion led him to be rewarded with the opportunity to watch the basketball royalty that was the Lakers for years.

That basketball is probably my most prized possession. I wouldn't sell it for a million dollars!

***

When 2010 rolled around, Alma became pregnant for the third time. Having had two girls, I figured I would be one of those dads to have three girls. And I was fine with that. As the pregnancy progressed, we came to the day when we were going to find out the sex of the baby.

As the nurse was performing the ultrasound, I noticed her stop, make a face, and then let out a slight "Hmm.". This is never a good sign at an ultrasound, but then she continued.

She smiled, pointed to the screen and said, "It's a boy."

I had tears of joy and Alma was crying when the nurse stepped out of the room. When she came back, she told us that the doctor wanted to see us.

We walked over to his office, where he explained that our son had an irregular heartbeat. Hearing this news, my own heart dropped and missed a few beats.

"Sometimes it goes away on its own," he explained. "Or Alma may need to be put on some medication to help correct the problem. But it's something we need to keep an eye on."

As the months passed, I tried not to worry about my son. Thankfully, I had a distraction in that 2010 was a great sports year for Los Angeles, as the Lakers won their 16th NBA Championship in June. It would be Kobe Bryant's fifth and final title. That kept me distracted for a while, until it was time for a follow-up visit with Alma's doctor.

Alma was informed that they would deliver our son via c-section.

"Great," I said. "What day?"

"August 23rd."

I laughed out loud. "August 23rd?"

Yup, August 23rd. Kobe Bryant's birthday. My son was going to be born on Kobe's birthday! My next thought was that we should name our son Kobe!

Alma wasn't too thrilled with that idea. In the end, we both agreed to Juan Carlos.

When the day came, I took my camcorder along to film so Melissa and Mariah could see the birth of their baby brother. While Alma got into her gown, I was given scrubs to wear, and I was once again faced with the familiar fear of uncertainty that was all too common for me.

As I took in my surroundings, I began questioning everything. It seems like there are more doctors than before; do they know something? Why are they looking like that? I don't remember that instrument from the last time!

I was staring at the mini chest shock machine—the ones they use when someone has a heart attack—and I thought, Why the hell do they have that here?

As they started the C-section, there was nothing I could do but rely on faith that everything would come out fine. I've been present at all three of my children's births, and the miracle of a baby being born never ceases to amaze me. I don't remember exactly how long we were in there, but when I saw Juan Carlos pulled out from Alma's stomach, I held my breath. I remember thinking, just cry please, Juan Carlos, just cry. In what seemed like an eternity, the doctors did their job, and I finally heard my son cry. It was the most beautiful cry I've ever heard!

Then he wouldn't stop crying.

The doctors became concerned. "Just talk to him," they said.

I held my son. "It's okay, Juan Carlos, I cooed. "It's okay. It's me, it's your dad."

And right then, right at that moment, Juan Carlos stopped crying. The screams in the room turned into silence.

The doctors laughed. "That did it," they said.

They took my son, while Alma and I went to her room, excited to tell the family the good news. When they got there, no one was more excited than the two new older sisters.

"We haven't signed anything yet," I told Alma. "Kobe is a great name.

Besides, this kid is long."

But Alma wasn't having it. I stepped out to run some errands, and when I returned, she told me that I had just missed the filing of the baby's name. She made me believe that I lost the opportunity to name him Kobe, and I was so bummed. She then handed me the copy.

Juan Carlos "Kobe" Catalan, born 8/23/2010.

Alma smiled. I was elated.

I've always said that someone who doesn't believe in God should watch a baby being born. I've witnessed three births, and every single time I was in complete awe. But the one great thing children give us is hope. If you have the right perspective, having a child should light a fire under you. They should make you want to be a better person and, ultimately, the best parent you can be.

Juan Carlos' smile can light up a room—the house and the next block. He can turn a bad day good.

Having been a girl dad for 12 years felt completely different to now having a son. I always said that I would teach my daughters right from wrong and try to lead them down the right path, but I could never teach them how to be women. That was on Alma. But with my son, not only do I have to lead him down the right path; I have to teach him how to be a man. A good man. An honest and strong man.

My dad was many things, and although he broke his back for his family, I never felt like I was given the rules of becoming a man from him—because I learned most of those rules on the streets the hard way. And some of those rules I learned wrong and had to unlearn them later.

Siblings can argue that parents have favorites, but I think the truth is parents get better with experience. You'll be a much better parent for child 3 or 4, compared to child 1 or 2. It's human nature to be critical or judgmental of how a person carries themselves or how they parent. We are all guilty of this. It's not until a person actually goes through hardships or experiences how a person was raised that they somewhat understand why a person is the way they are.

I think the more you love your kids, the better they feel about themselves, which allows them to deal with life issues in a better way. You give them confidence. Just knowing that you have someone in your corner is beyond comforting. And being prideful can ruin everything. Forgiveness is healing, and it's not about the individual deserving to be forgiven—it's the fact that the forgiveness is for you, not them. It doesn't mean you condone the person's actions; it's to rid you of the feelings of anger, hate, or resentment. You feel lighter and, believe me, with everything that life can throw at you, feeling those negative feelings is the last thing you want.

I think about my kids a lot. I wonder if I did this wrong, that wrong, and especially if I went overboard when I transferred my love of sports to them. Being a true sports fan means you ride with your team whether they are champions or the worst team in the league. While I can't explain the passion I feel for my teams, I can say that there is something that happens when your team wins. You didn't do anything. You weren't there. But you walk taller because of it.

Sports teaches us discipline, teamwork, and sportsmanship. Sports have the power to unite people. The effect that professional athletes have on people, especially kids, is a beautiful thing. Looking back now, I can see me growing up with depression and sadness, and I'm not exactly sure why, but the one constant through that loneliness has been sports. Sports won't abandon you; sports won't treat you badly, and sports won't turn its back on you.

I think of my favorite sports teams as part of my family. I cheer for them, I celebrate with them, I lose with them, and I'm sad with them. They're always with me through the good times and the bad times.

I took Juan Carlos to his first Dodger game when he was just one year old. I know he won't remember it, but I will. And I wanted him to know and feel the love I have for the Los Angeles Dodgers. It was five years later when I took him to his first NFL game. It was the Rams vs. 49ers, week 1 of the 2016 season.

I know a kid's attention span at six years old is not the best, and because I wanted JC to be engaged in the game, I bought some tickets in the first row on the 49ers home end zone. The day before we drove up to San Francisco, I got a couple things ready to bring along on our trip, one of them being an official NFL Speed helmet that I bought after my favorite player, Colin Kaepernick, wore it. Alma asked me why I was taking it, and I told her I was going to try and get it signed. Her response? "You are crazy."

Colin Kaepernick was the most dynamic quarterback I had ever seen. He was built like a linebacker and had a canon of an arm and the speed of a cheetah. Colin had us 49ers fans wowing everywhere, especially when he led the 49ers back to the Super Bowl. He made us all believers. He made me love football in a new way.

But when he started peacefully protesting the injustices we as a country are plagued with, it really struck a chord with me because I think I've experienced one of the worst possible injustices. He was a voice for the voiceless. Here in America, the greatest country in the world, whether it's designed that way or not, there are advantages and disadvantages for certain people based on the color of their skin. It's a story that seems to repeat itself over and over with little to no change.

Sadly, when Colin started speaking up, it was received with anger and hate. Somehow, people took his message as showing disrespect to our flag and armed forces. Now, I have taught my kids that they need to show respect to anyone who decides to put their lives on the line for the reason of protecting us and our country, just like I'd been taught when I was a kid. During my school years, we would recite the Pledge of Allegiance, the last words being "with liberty and justice for all." If you ask any reasonable or honest person if they believe this exists here in America, I think the answers would be all over the place.

The game we were at was the last game of week 1 and was scheduled to kick off at 7:20 p.m. I drove up to San Francisco with JC at about 7:00 a.m. We made the 5-hour drive and with a gas stop and a food stop, we got there around 1:30 p.m. We hung out for a little bit in our Tahoe, then made our way to the main gate, excited to be some of the first fans into Levi's Stadium. As we waited, there were a few fans who noticed I had an official 49er's helmet. When they asked why I brought it along, I told them I wanted to get it autographed, and they were also excited.

"That's awesome," they said. "I hope you get it signed."

I think people who are genuinely happy for other people are amazing. On the contrary, there are those who are the opposite. For example, a security guard noticed the helmet and asked why I brought it.

When I told him, he smirked. "You'll never get it signed."

Once the gates opened, I grabbed JC's hand, and we made our way to our seats, walking down the stairs to the first row by the 49er's tunnel.

Opening days in sports are some of my favorites as it's a new beginning, filled with hopes and endless possibilities. This day was no exception. We were there for only a few minutes when I heard someone from the field yell out.

"Hey," they said. "You want to come onto the field?"

Listening, I thought, wow, what a lucky person! Then, I heard it again, "You want to come onto the field?"

As I looked for who was talking, I saw that they were looking at us. This person had pointed to us!

"Yeah, you. Do you want to come onto the field with your son?"

I nearly passed out! Grabbed JC and, of course, the helmet, we practically ran toward the man, who met me and handed me two passes. I showed them to security, and before I knew it, we were on the field! I couldn't believe I was walking on the same field where my favorite team and football legends play! With JC on my right side and this stranger on my left, I was beside myself trying to keep it together as I told him that I was a diehard 49ers fan and thanked him profusely.

The players were working out on the field, while fans were hanging over the edge, yelling for their favorite players to come over for autographs. I was just excited to see any player, but when I looked to the left, who was making his way right to us? No one else but Colin Kaepernick. Now, mind you, I had played catch with my son since he was three or four years old, and we pretended we were both Kap! So, I was speechless to see Kap walking straight toward us.

My reaction was the same as when Todd met Kobe, and I just handed him my helmet—yes, I handed him my helmet! Somewhat confused, he looked at me and said, "Okay." Pulling a marker from my pocket, I handed it to him, and he signed the helmet and handed it back. I somehow managed to snap out of it long enough to tell him that he was my favorite player.

"Thank you," he said. "I appreciate that."

I then asked him if he could sign the Kaepernick jerseys JC and I both happened to be wearing. Colin couldn't have been any nicer and even took a picture with my son. I was so caught up in the moment that I forgot to take a picture with him myself!

I do remember a lot of media present that day, because Colin had started his peaceful kneeling earlier that preseason.

After our interaction, the gentleman who invited us down to the field told me it was time to walk off. I couldn't have done so any happier. As we walked toward the gate we came in through, I looked over to the man.

"Who are you?" I asked.

"My name is John Nguyen," he said.

"John," I said, "I don't know how to pay you back for this."

He just smiled.

I found out later that John owns a Volkswagen dealership up north and was a premier season ticket holder. He regularly did this, too. He picked out parents with their kids and invited them onto the field. God bless his heart.

As we walked back to our seats, I heard some fans screaming, which was odd being that it was still 90 minutes until the game started. I scanned the area for the yelling fans, and unbelievably it was the same fans, those same guys that were excited for me for me to get my helmet signed!

Other fans who also saw our interaction stopped us and wanted to take pictures with the helmet. Seeing this, reporters who were working Japanese television asked if I would agree to an interview because they saw me talking to Colin. I agreed, and the questions were about Colin's kneeling protest. I told them that Kap was my favorite NFL player and that my son and I had driven five hours from Los Angeles to see and support him. In addition, I told them that I stood side by side with Colin in his protest of racism and injustices that plague our great country, pointing out that Colin was using his platform to be a voice for the voiceless. I explained that he meant no disrespect toward our flag or armed services but rather was exercising our American right to protest peacefully.

The reporters thanked me and went on their way. Back at our seats, I just kept looking at the helmet.

The game couldn't have been any better! We shut out the St. Louis Rams, but that wasn't even the best part. Throughout the game, JC got the VIP treatment! The 49er's cheerleaders babied him, and Sourdough Sam, the team mascot, jumped into our seats and fired up the crowd. Later, he walked over to high five JC! Security guards surprisingly handed us drinks, and an NFL referee even walked over and handed JC a player-worn towel that one of the players had dropped! I still remember the fans that were sitting next to us asking, "Who are you guys?"

I've been to other memorable sporting events with my son, such as the 2017 World Series between the Los Angeles Dodgers and the Houston Cheaters, I mean Trashtros. It was game two, and what a game it was. We actually sat two rows behind where Corey Seager hit a homerun. It was a back-and-forth game that went into extra innings with the wrong team winning. Another memorable sporting event was JC's first Laker game, which happened to be Kobe's dual jersey retirement game. I had waited to take him to a Lakers game because I wanted him to be old enough to pay attention and get into the game. I paid an arm and a leg for four tickets to watch this legendary moment of the Black Mamba! From the opening tip to the end of the game, which went into overtime, JC 's eyes were glued on the court. I still remember him asking me when Kobe was going to play, and I told him Kobe was no longer playing, but his jersey was being retired because he was such an amazing player.

We also attended the next year's 2018 World Series between the Dodgers and Boston Red Sox. I took JC to game three here at Dodger Stadium, and little did we know we would be watching two games in one as the game went 18 innings! The best part was that we won the game with a Max Muncy walk-off home run, but JC wanted to leave the game around the 8th inning! I had to use my oratorical skills to keep him calm and patient—and some ice cream and candy, of course! Fast forward to the present, JC LOVES going to a 49ers game, followed by Laker games, and last, I pretty much have to beg him to join me for a Dodger game, which makes me sad. As far as him playing sports, it is almost in the same order. I signed him up for three seasons of baseball, but he says he doesn't like the lack of action in the game. He has not played football yet, even though he wants to, but his mom and sisters do not want him to because of the heavy hitting. Now, basketball?—he has played four or five seasons, and he is hooked on basketball!

Yes!

***

In 2012, Todd called.

"Hey, some guy from New York wants to come out and talk to us about possibly making a movie about your story."

"What? That's crazy."

"Yeah, but it could be fun," he said.

So I agreed.

A man named Jacob LaMendola flew out and met with us over the weekend. Jacob told us he had been fascinated with the case ever since he'd heard about it. Both Todd and I shared our perspective of the events surrounding the murder case. It was a good conversation, and he thanked us for our time and said he would go back and talk to his team and get back to us. I thought it went well. We heard back from him quickly, and he told us he wanted to create a documentary or a 90-minute film.

Cool.

In 2013, we were flown to New York to film.

Ever since I was a kid, I've been nervous when I speak to strangers. My mind blanks out, and I lose all train of thought. So, on the first day of filming, I walked over to a quiet corner in that noisy and busy studio, and I prayed. I asked God to give me the thoughts and words to portray an honest and genuine account of the events.

We met the filmmaking team. and over the next four days, we shot the interviews.

When I was first put in front of that camera, it took a few times before I was able to show the raw emotion you see in the documentary. But I got there. My favorite part was after my interviews when I was just listening to Todd's perspective of the case, because I can literally listen to him talk about law all day long.

We wrapped up, got to enjoy a little of New York, and then headed back to Los Angeles.

It took five years for the documentary to be complete and released. We received updates on other interviews as they took place. Back and forth we went with the filming team; add this, remove that, etc. Contrary to belief, I didn't get paid to do the documentary. I was told that since it was not acting but rather a "documentary," I couldn't be. Netflix joining the project in the end was a surprise that was added to strengthen the film. They were the ones to officially classify the documentary into the short documentary category.

As we waited for the release on September 29, 2017, my family and I were granted a sneak peek the day before.

It wasn't long after the documentary aired that I started receiving positive feedback, first from family and friends, then from local people I didn't know. Then messages from around the world began coming in, including places that I had only heard of in a classroom.

These messages talked about fate and God watching over me. People were saying that every time they watched the documentary, they learned something new. I also received nonstop questions, asking what I'm doing next. Would I make a real movie based on a true story, or a series?

"A book," I answered.

"Yeah?" people responded. "A book would be great."

This book.

***

I have been criticized for attempting to return to school. I'm not really sure why, maybe when people cannot do something, they want to let you know that you can't do it, either. And I know school does not guarantee success, but it sure helps to prepare in whatever field you are interested in. Have I had self-doubt? Absolutely, but I made a choice that I would not allow fear or self-doubt to dictate my life. I just figured if my life ends, well, it will end with me putting forth my best effort.

Even though I was the subject in "Longshot," which was as raw as you can get emotionally, there is something in me that makes me believe like I can totally do acting—isn't that weird? In college, the theatre classes amazed me, and that bug stayed in there.

Being on social media fueled that, as you want to share all your experiences through pictures and stories. Add that up with being able to follow your favorite celebrities and athletes, and you will find yourself surfing social media for hours. Now, I have never considered myself famous—I believe I have an important story to tell—but having people reach out because of the documentary has been a surprise, and it got me thinking. That said, there are some requests that stand out more than others.

Being born in Los Angeles, our culture is recognized worldwide. One DM that came in was from the clothing brand "Born x Raised" and its founder, who went by the name Spanto. He told me a little bit about himself and his clothing brand and what it stood for. He mentioned that he came across the documentary and that it resonated with him since he'd lived through the L.A. street life. I didn't know about the brand, but as I learned about it and wore some of the clothing, I became a big fan. The original designs and quality spoke for themselves.

We went back and forth, sharing each other's background and our mutual love for the Dodgers, and I was completely surprised when he asked me if I would be interested in doing a photoshoot for his latest Dodger clothing drop. He also asked if my daughter would be interested in joining in the shoot. I asked Melissa, and she was really excited … but nervous.

He called me on a September, 2020 right in the middle of the pandemic, and we agreed to do the photoshoot at Angel's Point, which is a small hill in Elysian Park that overlooks Dodger Stadium and has an amazing view. We pulled up and after hugging it out, we went right into the photoshoot. As we took photos, we talked about that fateful day and learned more about each other. I also brought along and wore the Kevin Brown jersey I wore that night at Dodger

Stadium.

Spanto was elated. He even took some videos of the encounter, which was cool. Then, when it came time to wrap up, we took some group photos, though I don't know who actually took them. Since we were in the middle of the pandemic, we were not sure if we should take photos with our masks on. It was then that Spanto mentioned that if he did not wear a mask, his wife, Anna, would annihilate him. This is when I learned that Spanto was a cancer survivor and was considered a high-risk individual during the pandemic.

The new Dodger merchandise dropped on September 18, 2020, and it sold out within minutes. It was not because of me; it was just that all the Dodger drops were super popular. However, I do think they might have been best sellers out of all his collaborations.

The next month, which was October, it just so happened that the Dodgers made it back to the World Series. Since the World Series was in Arlington, during Covid, I flew out to Dallas with two of my cousins just to witness the Dodgers possibly clinching the championship. I took my BxR 1988 Championship hat that Spanto gave me, hoping we would win it all. Sure enough, the Dodgers finally pulled it off, and the celebration was insane. I sent Spanto the picture when we clinched it and told him that the photoshoot we took was the reason we won it all, and he agreed, ha-ha. We kept in contact over the months for a span of about three years. Although we always tried to get together, to have a beer or just to chill and talk, it just didn't happen.

Still, we texted back and forth over the next several months. If I ever forgot to reach out, he always checked in on me to see how I was doing. Finally, in April 2022, he texted me and asked if I was going to the game, and I told him I was. About midway through the game, Spanto texted me to meet him behind home plate field level. Man, were we excited to see each other! We chopped it up a bit, and when I asked him who he was with, I was surprised when he said he was with Mr. Cartoon!

Anyone who knows about tattoos knows the name Mr. Cartoon. He is a legend here in Los Angeles and around the globe. He has tattooed just about everyone who is famous! Spanto asked me if I wanted to meet him, to which I replied, "Hell, yeah!" Back at the seats, I met Cartoon and his wife, and we ended up taking one of the coolest pictures I have ever taken. Two legends and me. Spanto mentioned something about hanging out after the game, so I left and headed back to my seat.

As I was leaving the Stadium, Spanto texted and said that he was going over to the Holiday Bar on Whittier Boulevard in Boyle Heights and wanted to know if I wanted to roll through. I asked my friend, Rolie, who was with me, if we were game to swing by and he said yes. Rolie knew about BxR before I did, and he is a long-time loyal customer.

When we arrived at the bar, we were greeted by the actual owner, who was super cool and as welcoming as a person can be. Spanto was with his older son, as well as Mr. Cartoon, and we spent the next couple of hours talking sports, family, and fate.

"I know this is weird—," I started, and Cartoon just smiled.

Being from L.A., I had known who Cartoon was since I was a kid. I was also a fan of the Netflix documentary called LA Originals, which chronicles the life of Cartoon and Estevan Oriol through the importance of photography, tattoos, and art and the role they played in what is known as the West Coast culture. And I remember thinking that if I were to ever get a serious tattoo, the only person I would let do it would be Mr. Cartoon.

In the same way Spanto told me he was able to relate to my situation, I also was able to see myself in him. We both grew up with tough childhoods and grew up byproducts of our environment. We got caught up in the system, whether by choice or fate. We both had children at a very young age, but by the grace of God, we were able to get somewhat straightened out to become positive role models and provide for our families. But I think the thing I saw about myself in Spanto the most was that he was a storyteller, like me. Ironically, I never thought of myself as a storyteller—that is, until my friend, Reed Adler, mentioned it. Like the artist that he was, Spanto had a way of describing or expressing exactly what he was thinking or seeing, whether it was words, art, or designing clothes. I've had an idea for a clothing line, which reflects my Hispanic roots and Los Angeles, and I wanted to pick Spanto's brain, but I was stupidly embarrassed to ask. Unfortunately, Spanto was involved in a bad car accident in New Mexico, and he passed in June of 2023. My heart went out to his beautiful family. Rest in power loco.

***

Around the year 2000, my dad was entertaining the idea of passing over the family business to me and my brother. Aat the time, Mario was 23, and I was 22 years old. Mario was a natural at the machine shop. He loved math and geometry, which sums up machine shop, numbers, and angles. My dad taught us on what are called manual mills and lathe machines, which means you move the dials to cut the metal or plastic according to your specifications on your blueprint. When I say this was a family business, it was a family business. We had uncles, cousins, nephews, and friends who worked there. Some things I admired most about my dad were his hard work ethic, level headedness, and perseverance he's shown since coming to the United States as an illegal immigrant. He followed the law ever since and ending up gaining legal citizenship about 20 years ago and is now an American citizen.

My dad has never believed in laziness, dishonesty, or using fraud to get ahead in life. I consider him to be one of the hardest workers alive. He has literally worked for SEVENTY YEARS! When someone suggested we should incorporate the business, we found someone who made our shop an S-Corporation, with my brother being named president and me a secretary, while our dad was behind the scenes.

Because my brother was the next one in charge after my dad, I just followed orders. His hope was that we would take over the business and make it grow. Since my dad only knew of manual machines, my brother and I thought we should look at new technology, which was CNC Machining. Computer numerical control (CNC) is a leaner, more efficient way of manufacturing parts using precision machine tools through automation and computer software. When one of my dad's associates was thinking about retiring, he offered him all his CNC equipment at what seemed like a reasonable price. We went ahead with the deal and started our new journey in computer machining.

We went on for a couple years and even upgraded our equipment to replace the older machines. Mario was always about making more money and felt that we were not making enough. My brother always found a way to make ends meet, even if it was not always legal. Before his eventual arrest, I often tried to talk to him to leave the illegal things and do the right things. I wanted him to apply himself more at the family business, but he thought easy money was the better route.

***

The day before graduation, Mel—my daughter, Melissa—wanted to capture some campus photos, so we arranged a shoot with Oscar and Wendy from Imagery by Oscar, a talented photography couple who always do an amazing job. We met by the CSUN sign in front of the school and began snapping away. Melissa looked beautiful, as always, and I ... well, I looked alright. We roamed the campus, visiting spots I had never ventured to during my time there, taking loving shots of the two of us together. We even found a classroom and an auditorium where we'd taken classes side by side, and of course, we had to get photos there, too.

I had always wanted to take pictures during class for memories, but Melissa, ever the modest one, would always say, "No, Dad, that's embarrassing!"

The week leading up to graduation was emotional, to say the least. One moment, I turned to Alma and said, "When we took those photos looking at each other, I was suddenly taken back in time, and I saw Melissa as my little girl again. I couldn't believe it. I've watched her graduate from grade school, middle school, high school—and now, here we are, graduating from CSUN together."

It had been a journey full of sleepless nights, hours of studying, research, writing, presentations, midterms, finals, frustration, tears— both good and bad. And it all led to this moment. Graduation day. As we stood there, together, as Business Management graduates, I couldn't help but feel that a dream had come true.

We'd stayed up late preparing the night before, only to wake up at 5 a.m. to get ready. I walked into Melissa's room while she was getting ready and asked how she was feeling. "Can you believe this is happening?" She replied, "No, not until it happens."

I told her, "I never in a million years imagined we'd be graduating together. What movie is that?!" But as I said it, I couldn't help but feel an overwhelming sense of pride. I was proud of her—not just for this incredible achievement, but for blossoming into such a beautiful, independent woman. On our drive to campus, she asked me what my favorite part of the journey had been. I thought for a moment and said, "It was probably the journey itself." I told her how I had struggled in community college, with a GPA of just 2.6, and that I never thought I'd make it this far. But by the time I was finishing up at CSUN, I had raised my GPA to 3.0. I didn't even realize how much I'd changed, how much I'd grown. What really made it all worthwhile, though, was sharing the finish line with her.

We arrived at CSUN with my parents and my niece, Desiree, following close behind. We rushed through security and made our way to the stands, where my family was already gathering. Todd was heading over, and the rest of our extended family would join us shortly. Once inside, I helped Melissa find our line (Business Management), and as we stood there, I began seeing for classmates I recognized. We joked about our time in class, whether the courses were tough or easy, and shared stories about our professors. The music started, and I could feel the adrenaline kick in, as if we were gearing up for a sporting event. The crowd was buzzing with energy.

I was getting compliments from strangers about the Kobe logo I had customized onto my sash. I needed that "Mamba Mentality" to get me here—no doubt about it. We sat down and scanned the crowd for our family, found them, and posed for pictures. The ceremony stretched on, and it felt like our names would never be called. It was a four-hour event, and we didn't walk until almost three hours in.

Finally, it was showtime.

Melissa and I made our way to the stage, and the emotions hit me like a wave. The next 30 seconds were a blur. All I remember is hearing Melissa's name called and, somehow, not hearing mine. I was caught up in the moment, in the flow of it all. I crossed the stage, shook hands with the President of the University, Erika D. Beck, and it felt like everything I had worked for was coming to fruition.

Afterward, chaos erupted as friends and family rushed to find their graduates. Melissa and I walked to our left, and there was Todd, waiting for us. We embraced in one of the biggest hugs we've ever shared. My family gathered around, congratulating us. There were photos, lots of pictures—my kids, my parents, Melissa and Mariah. Mariah even suggested we recreate the moment I was released from jail when I picked Todd up, as shown in the documentary. But this time, Todd was the one picking me up. That moment was epic.

After the ceremony, we were all exhausted and hungry, so we headed to one of my favorite spots, Nat's Café, in Canoga Park. The random strangers who congratulated us felt like a blessing, reminding me just how far we'd come. We ate, chatted, and then hurried home to finish setting up for the celebration.

By 5 p.m., I was already scrambling. The original invitation said the party would start at 5, but we changed it to 6. My friend, Russ, showed up at 5:45. Half-jokingly, I said, "What the hell, Russ?" He responded, "I thought I was late!"

As the party ramped up, I took it easy, making sure to talk to everyone and make them feel welcome. We had a taco stand, a DJ, and even a live band. Little by little, guests arrived. I was thrilled to see some familiar faces, including OG Carnal, a fellow diehard 49er fan who is super popular on social media and who I happened to meet at a road game in Miami. He and his brothers-in-law, Francisco, and Rigo, drove three and a half hours just to celebrate with us. That's what good friends do.

As the night wore on, the taco people wanted to pack up, but the band was still playing. I saw an opportunity to make my speech. I'd been wanting to speak from the heart, but in the moment, my nerves got the best of me. My mind went blank, and I was disappointed with my speech. Now, the beautiful part about writing is that it gives you the chance to keep going until you get it right.

So here's what I really wanted to say:
"Thank you, everyone, for being here tonight. Very few people know what I've been through, what I've suffered, or what I've endured. But

on this night, I choose to focus on the good. I'm grateful. So grateful. Not everyone has both their parents alive. I do, and for that, I thank God. Dad, thank you for showing me what it means to work hard and honestly. Mom, thank you for always loving me and comforting me, no matter what. To my sisters, Gabby, Patty, and Nidia—I've always wanted to be a good brother to you and set the right example. Alma, thank you for giving me three amazing children. Melissa, I'm beyond proud of you. Thank you for setting the example for your siblings. Mariah, continue to work hard and I can't wait to celebrate your accomplishments. Juan Carlos, keep dreaming big, son, and just remember you can do anything you set your mind to. To everyone who has helped me along the way, your support has meant the world. And a special shout-out to OG Carnal and his brothers-in-law for making the long drive to celebrate with us. You're a real one. Finally, to Todd—thank you. I love you like a brother. You've impacted my life in so many positive ways. I look up to you. I've tried to follow your example so I can make you proud."

Raising my glass, I would propose a toast: "To hard work, accomplishing goals, and a happy and prosperous life."

The celebration continued into the early hours of the morning, but by 1 a.m., I was wiped out. We went to bed after an unforgettable week. The next day, I woke up and asked Melissa, "Did you have fun last night?" She replied, "Dad, I had a BLAST!"

As the day unfolded, we opened gifts—Dodger gear, fine bottles of alcohol, and, of course, graduation cards. I was overwhelmed by the kind words. One card in particular, from Melissa's friends, said, "Thank you for raising such a wonderful person like Melissa." That hit me like a ton of bricks. To be told your child is a good person is the ultimate compliment a parent can receive.

As I reflect on this chapter of my life, I feel like the life I've always wanted is only just beginning. I'm putting my new degree to work and building my future—an organic Mezcal line, a clothing brand, all reflecting Los Angeles and our West Coast culture.

This is just the beginning.

So the Dodgers with two out in the ninth inning buried under a seven run ninth by Atlanta. Gary Sheffield certainly the player of the game. I mean he got a base hit to drive in a run, and stole a base so the Dodgers walked him three times. When they pitched to him again in the ninth inning, he doubled in two, and he's made two very fine catches in right field. Meanwhile, David Ross coming up, and he will bat for Cabrerra, and lifts it into left field. Chipper Jones is there. And --- that'll do it. So the Braves break open what was a wonderful game for eight innings, 4-4, Gary Sheffield comes back to haunt the Dodgers. Bong is the winning pitcher; the loser is Eric Gagne. One of those rare nights in the life of one of the premier relievers in the league. Tomorrow night, game two of the three game series, that'll be Russ Ortiz and Kaz Ishii. We certainly hope you make your plans to be with us. I'd like to remind you that then Wednesday, Greg Maddux and Kevin Brown. Once again, the final score, Braves 11, Dodgers 4. For Ross Porter and Rick Monday, this is Vince Scully saying so long from Dodgers Stadium.

Vin Scully, Dodger's Stadium, May 12, 2003

CONCLUSION
WRITTEN BY MELISSA CATALAN

My name is Melissa Marie Catalan, daughter of Juan Catalan. I was born on December 27, 1997. As I write these final words for this book—my father's book—I realize it is not just a story of injustice or perseverance. It is a story about love. About family. About the quiet strength of a man who refused to be broken.

One of my earliest memories of my dad was from elementary school, receiving awards for academics. There he was, smiling ear to ear, holding balloons. Always balloons. Always there. Always proud. It used to make me shy—maybe even embarrassed—but looking back, I see how lucky I was. That wasn't just a father showing up; it was a man pouring love into every single moment he had with his daughter.

But life wasn't always filled with balloons and assembly awards. There were dark moments, too—confusing, painful ones. I was too young to understand everything when my dad was taken away. I remember wanting him home more than anything. I remember the Halloween we dressed up and stood in line at the jail, hoping to show him our costumes—only to be told we couldn't see him. That memory still stings.

And yet, even as a child, I learned that strength isn't always loud. Sometimes it's found in a courtroom, in the voice of a six-year-old girl mustering the courage to speak up for her father. With my uncle by my side, and my favorite doll in my arms, I testified—because I wanted my dad home.

When his name was finally cleared, I didn't fully grasp the magnitude of what that meant. But today, as a grown woman, I know it was the day the truth prevailed—and our family could be reunited.

Years later, I watched my father type and type, pouring out his soul onto a laptop. He was working, going to school, raising us—yet still determined to write his book. At first, I thought he was crazy. But then he began reading me parts of it. I could hear how powerful his story was. I saw how determined he remained, even when he was exhausted. That's who my father is: he keeps going. No matter what.

I was lucky enough to attend college with him. Even luckier to sit in the same classrooms. We shared notes, studied together, and helped each other through challenging times. When my anxiety or dizzy spells made it hard to show up, he was there—his presence grounding me. I may have thought I'd be helping him, but it was really the other way around. Just like always.

On May 17, 2025, we walked the graduation stage together, side by side. Same school. Same major. Same dream. It was more than a milestone; it was a moment like no other. After the ceremony, he threw a party—just for me, because he knew how much it meant. He's always done that—putting others first, even when he didn't feel like celebrating himself.

As I continue running my own small business and working toward opening a nail salon of my own, I do so carrying every lesson he taught me: to work hard, to never give up, to believe in something greater. He showed me what resilience looks like—not through grand gestures, but through the quiet power of showing up every day, no matter what life throws at you.

This book matters because his story matters. Because others need to know that even in the face of injustice, hope can survive. That you can rebuild a life—and even make it beautiful. That love, family, and truth have the power to rise above it all.

If I could say just one thing about my dad, it would be this: He is the strongest, most hardworking, dedicated, and optimistic man I've ever known. As I write this, tears run down my face—not from sadness, but from gratitude. God truly blessed my siblings and me with an amazing father, a protector, and a leader.

He deserves all the great things in life. And with this book, I hope the world sees that, too.

   —Melissa Marie Catalan

ABOUT THE AUTHOR
WRITTEN BY MELISSA CATALAN

Juan Catalan is a graduate of California State University, Northridge, with a Bachelor's degree in Business Management. He is the owner and president of Catalan Machining, a family-run business built on resilience, hard work, and legacy. A lifelong collector of sports cards and memorabilia, Juan sees value not just in objects, but in the stories they tell.

Beyond business, he is passionate about personal growth, health, education, travel, and leaving a meaningful mark on the world. But above all, he is a proud father of three—his greatest inspiration and the heart behind everything he does. Juan's journey is one of perseverance, purpose, and a relentless drive to turn life's challenges into opportunities for impact.

PLAYED

JUAN CATALAN

THE DAY
I MET KOBE

AFTER THE MAVERICKS GAME IN 2005.

THE
DAY I MET

MAGIC JOHNSON, 2013.

MY TIO TOMAS

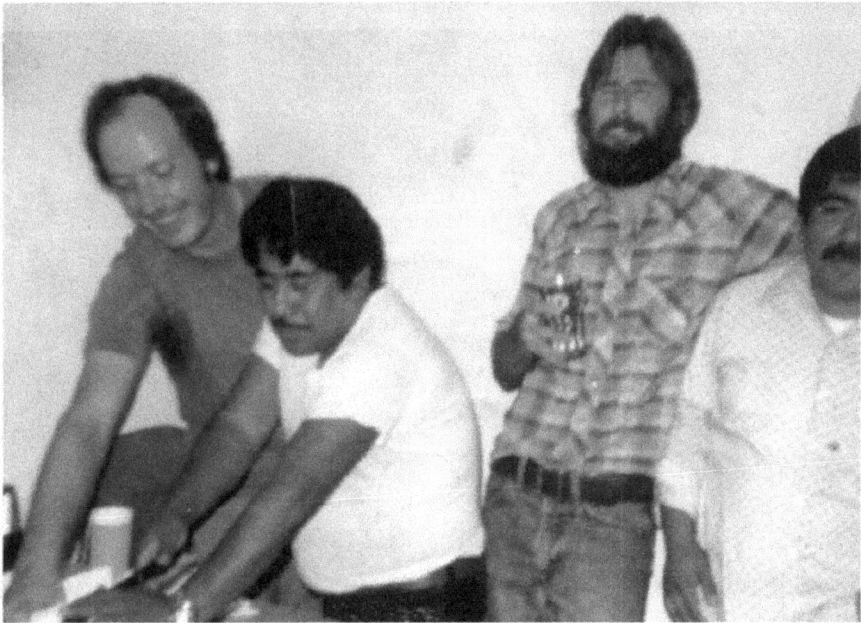

SECOND FROM THE LEFT.

THE DAY
I MET DR JERRY BUSS

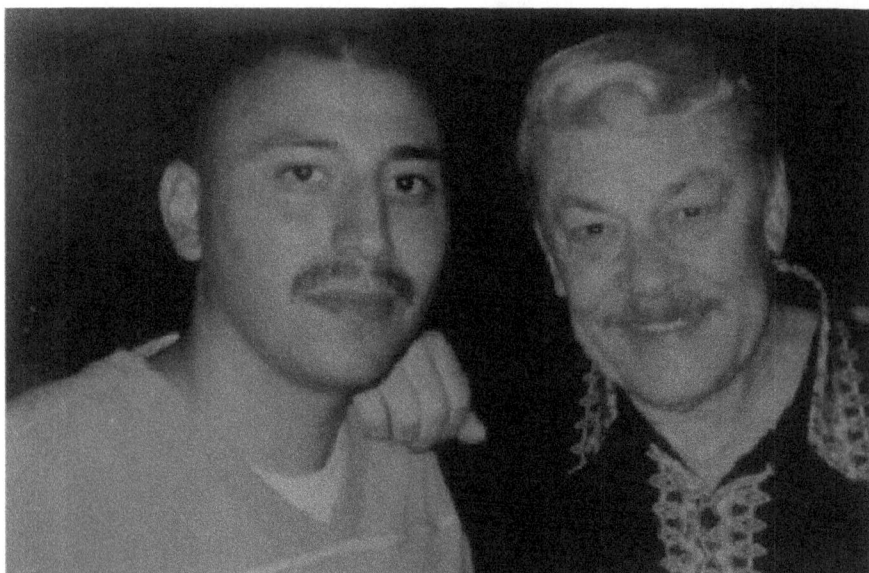

AFTER THE 2004 NBA FINALS GAME 2
(JUNE, 2004).

MY SON
JUAN CARLOS

LOOKING UP
TO ME IN 2012.

MEETING
COLIN KAEPERNICK

AT JC'S FIRST
NFL GAME.

ME WITH
MY GODPARENTS

AT MY FIRST
COMMUNION, 1990.

TODD AND I IN NEW YORK

WITH THE STATUE OF LIBERTY,
2017.

JUAN CARLOS
AND I AT THE DODGERS

WORLD SERIES, OCTOBER 2018.

TODD AND
I AT THE DODGERS

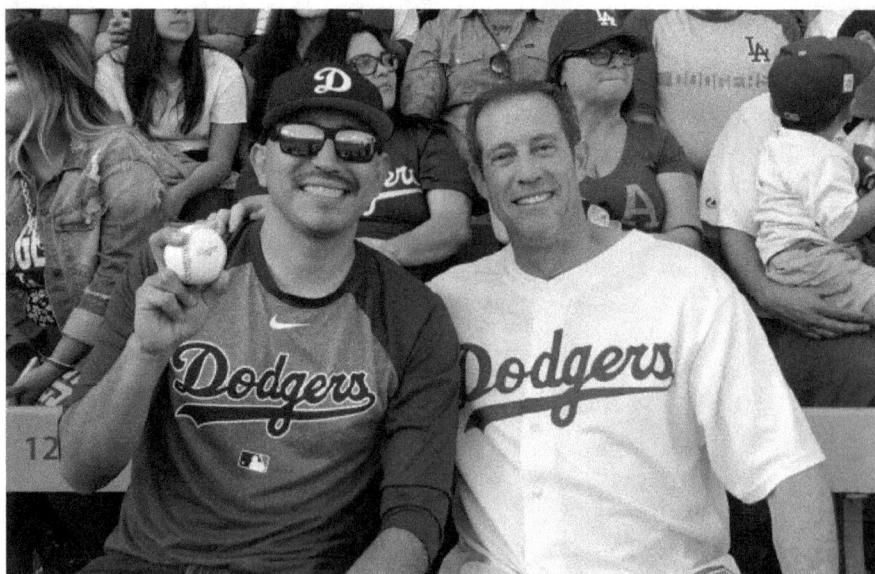

WORLD SERIES IN 2018.

JUAN CARLOS
AND I AT A LAKERS GAME

IN MARCH, 2019.

JUAN CARLOS AND I ON THE FIELD

AT LEVI'S STADIUM THE DAY WE MET COLIN KAEPERNICK.

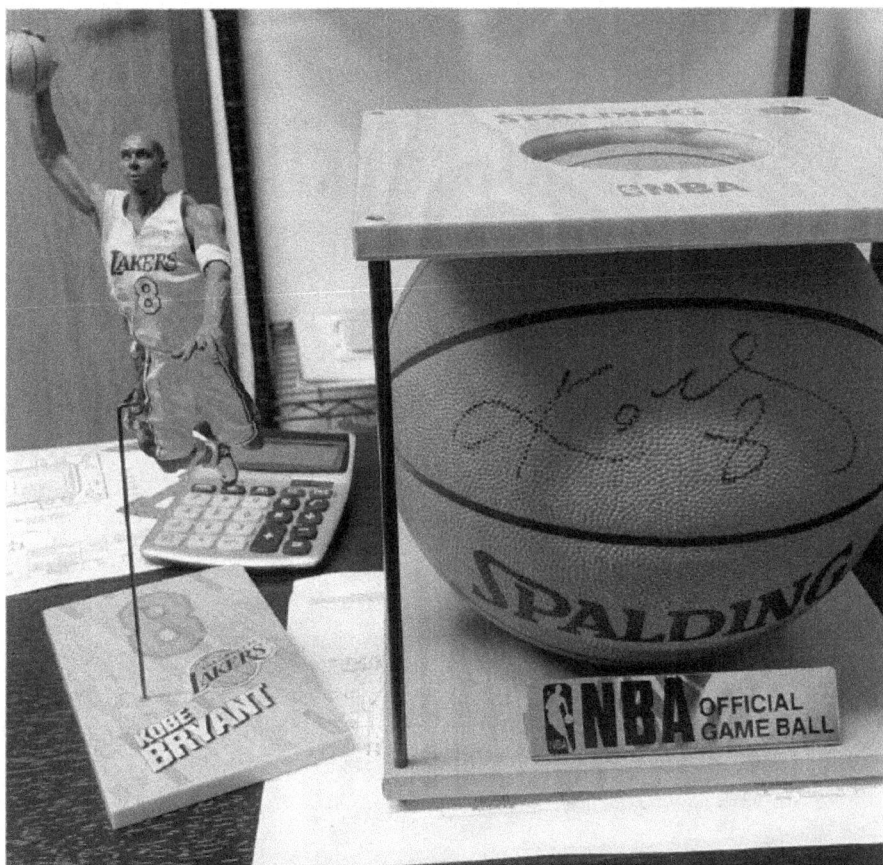

THE AUTOGRAPHED KOBE BASKETBALL

THAT TODD GIFTED ME FOR CHRISTMAS, DECEMBER, 2005.

THE ENGLISH TEXTBOOK FROM MY FIRST SEMESTER AT

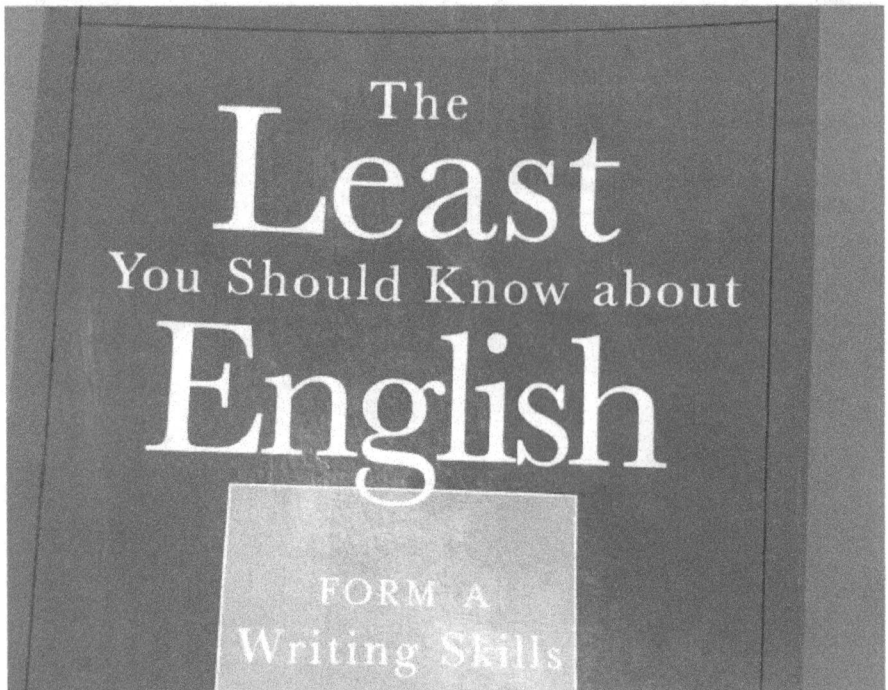

The
Least
You Should Know about
English

FORM A
Writing Skills

PIERCE COLLEGE IN WOODLAND HILLS, CALIFORNIA.

EXERCISES

Put parentheses around the prepositional phrases in the following sentence
Be sure to start with the preposition itself (*in, on, to, at, of. . .*) and include t
word or words that go with it (*in the morning, on our sidewalk, to Hawaii . .*
Then underline the sentences' subjects once and verbs twice. Remember th
subjects and verbs are not found inside prepositional phrases, so if you loca
the prepositional phrases *first*, the subjects and verbs will be much easier
find. Review the answers given at the back for each set of ten sentences befo
continuing.

Exercise 1

1. A day (at a baseball game) is always fun.
2. (For one man,) a day (at a baseball game) proved his innocence.
3. Juan Catalan went to (a Dodger game (with his girlfriend.)
4. (On that day,) a TV show filmed one (of its episodes.)
5. Unfortunately, on (that same day (in Los Angeles,) a terrible cri
   occurred.
6. Later, the police arrested Juan Catalan (as a suspect (in the murder c
   and put him (in jail.)
7. Catalan's girlfriend remembered the filming (of the TV show (at the ga
   (on the day (of the murder,)
8. Officials reviewed the footage (of the *Curb Your Enthusiasm* show (fr
   that day (at Dodger Stadium.)
9. (In the background (of one (of the outtakes,) Catalan and his girlfri
   appear clearly (in the stands (next to Larry David,) the star (of the sho
10. (After the discovery (of undeniable proof (of his alibi,) the police relea
    Juan Catalan.

Source: Newsweek, June 14, 2004

Exercise 2

1. The many cases (of food poisoning (in America) each year alarm peo
2. Some food scientists point (to food irradiation (as one possible soluti
3. The irradiation (of food) kills bacteria (through exposure (to gamma r

FAMILY PORTRAIT BACK

IN 2010.

DON FRANCISCO AND I AT HIS TALK SHOW DON FRANCISCO PRESENTA

IN MIAMI, 2004.

ME BACK
IN THE DAY

IN LITTLE
LEAGUE.

ME AND MY
BROTHER WITH
MOM AND DAD

IN THE
EARLY 1980S.

ME AS
A BABY

WITH MOM.

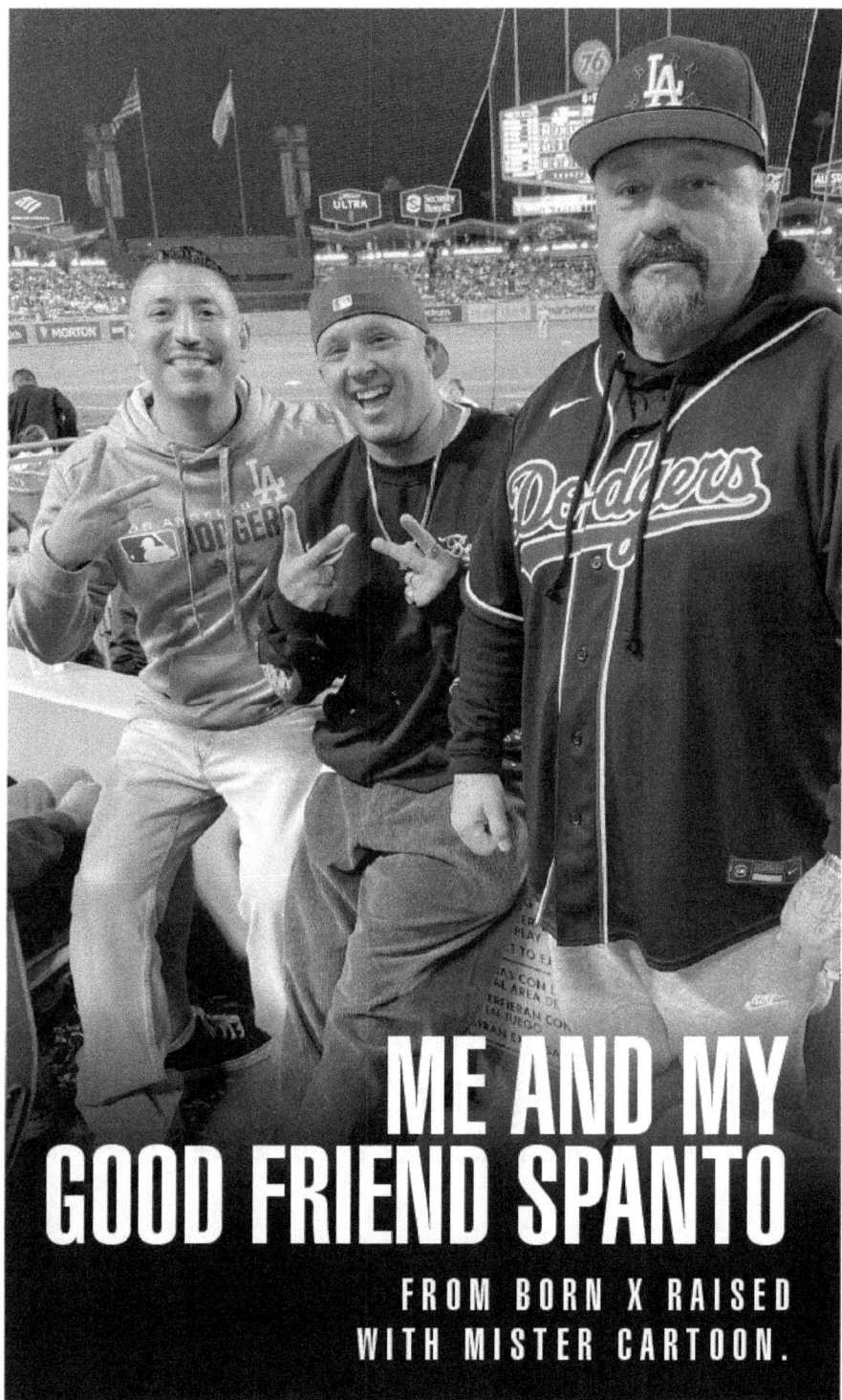

ME AND MY GOOD FRIEND SPANTO

FROM BORN X RAISED WITH MISTER CARTOON.

AT MY GRANDPARENTS HOUSE WITH MY FATHER AND TIO NACHO
(BOTTOM LEFT TO RIGHT).

THIS IS ME WITH MY TWO COUSINS LUÍS
AND CAMILO (LEFT TO RIGHT)

MELISSA AND I AT THE BORN X RAISED

PHOTOSHOOT DURING COVID, 2020.

TODD AND I

THE DAY I WAS
RELEASED FROM JAIL

AND THE DAY
I RECEIVED

MY BACHELORS DEGREE IN BUSINESS
FROM CAL STATE NORTHRIDGE

MELISSA AND I GRADUATING TOGETHER

FROM CSUN, (CALIFORNIA STATE UNIVERSITY OF NORTHRIDGE).

www.ingramcontent.com/pod-product-compliance
Lightning Source LLC
Chambersburg PA
CBHW062128020426
42335CB00013B/1145